ANNE LAIDLAW

KICK ADDICTION by Anne Laidlaw
Published by Creation House
A Strang Company
600 Rinehart Road
Lake Mary, Florida 32746
www.creationhouse.com

Publisher's Note: The views expressed in this book are not necessarily the views held by the publisher.

Unless otherwise noted, all Scripture quotations are from the New King James Version of the Bible. Copyright © 1979, 1980, 1982 by Thomas Nelson, Inc., publishers. Used by permission. Scripture quotations marked NIV are from the Holy Bible, New International Version. Copyright © 1973, 1978, 1984, International Bible Society. Used by permission.

Front cover photo is for illustrative purposes only.

Cover design by Terry Clifton

Library of Congress Control Number: 2006936892

International Standard Book Number-10: 1-59979-154-4
International Standard Book Number-13: 978-1-59979-154-8

First Edition
07 08 09 10 11 — 987654321
Printed in the United States of America

It is a pleasure to endorse Anne's new title *Kick Addiction*. I highly favor guides that offer the truth of the Word of God to those who are willing to renew their minds to the Word, believe, and act accordingly.

—Dick B.
Active recovered AA
author of thirty titles on
AA's Bible roots, Christian fellowship, and cures
Kihei, Hawaii

A masterly distillation of the truth needed to find freedom. Scriptural, practical, confrontational, and releasing. An awesome help to find God's way. Real truth to experience the freedom life God has prepared for all of us to walk in. Thank you, Anne.

—Cam Rimmer
Director of Living Waters
New Zealand

Acknowledgments

Thank you, Anna, for inspiring me to write this book. Special thanks also to Bruce Kemp for your ongoing encouragement and insights, Jayne Calkin for your inspired suggestions about the manuscript, and Allen Quain and the team at Strang for their help in making this a reality. My love and thanks also overflow to my three children, Jacob, Rachael, and Danielle, without whose love, support, patience, and continual encouragement this book would never have been written. May the glory go to Jesus Christ, who has made Himself so real in our lives.

CONTENTS

INTRODUCTION

*The chains of habit are too weak to be felt
until they are too strong to be broken.*[1]
—SAMUEL JOHNSON

No one wants to be an addict! A fourteen-year-old young man doesn't add to his list of life goals, "Become an addict by the time I'm twenty-one." A woman doesn't dream of being twenty pounds overweight ten years from now. A fifty-year-old man does not set a goal of masturbating in front of pornographic movies. It just sort of "happens." Small, seemingly insignificant choices are made one after the other. Each choice may be ignorantly chosen, but every one is mightily fruitful, and the end results are life changing, for better or worse.

It usually starts with a legitimate desire, such as a need for love, attaching itself to a behavior, thing, or person in an attempt to find fulfillment. For example, you may experience a deep feeling of satisfaction with the first flush of alcohol in a social setting, making you feel open and available for intimacy. The connection is made and every time the behavior or thought is repeated and reinforced it becomes stronger and stronger, slowly developing into a habit and then an addiction. Eventually you begin to feel unable to cope in social settings without alcohol. Or perhaps a sense of being loved and gaining approval may become attached to your mother's delight in her shoes. For it is when she is buying new shoes or trying them on that she is most animated, and in your need for acceptance, you, her only son, slowly develop a shoe fetish.

Addiction usually starts with a longing for fulfillment of a legitimate desire or need, because we all do have legitimate desires and needs. However, we often go to the wrong place, in a naive attempt to have them fulfilled. We go to broken cisterns that have no ability to fulfill what they seem to promise. God recognizes our tendency to do this and He clearly labels and judges this behavior. "For My people have committed two evils: They have forsaken Me, the fountain of living waters, And hewn themselves cisterns—broken cisterns that can hold no water" (Jer. 2:13). However, He also knows our basic needs are real, for He placed them within us.

What Are These Basic Needs?

We all need *unconditional love*, but we won't find the real thing in the arms of a prostitute, through infidelity, or trying to please everyone. We won't even find it through our children. Initially it should come from our parents and then, as we mature, be transferred on to our Father in heaven. But sadly, our parents aren't perfect, and none of us received perfect unconditional love from them. Instead we are more likely to receive greater wounds and complex defense mechanisms that make us less likely to turn to God for help, and make it more difficult to trust anyone.

In our need for unconditional love, we long to feel we are valued for who we are, not just for what we do. Yet how many of us were rejected if we misbehaved as children, or are still rejected if we don't live up to others' expectations? Sadly, most people are too caught up in how they feel to have any regard for the feelings of others.

We all need a sense of *security* and we won't find this at the racecourse, lottery, in our bank account balance, educational degrees, our rich spouse, through peer approval, or even within ourselves. We long to know that if the gravel vanished beneath our feet we are not solely left to our own resources, because deep down we know how incapable we are! We know how hard it would be to cope if everything we relied on collapsed. Many have even found out!

Finally, we all need to know our lives have *significance* and *purpose* and that we aren't here just to push up the petunias. Life isn't a meaningless slog from morning to night, year in, year out, from playpen to playschool, flat, home, and then a rocking chair in a rest home. Yet we won't find this significance in our work, relationships, or even our creativity. It may feel like we have found it temporarily, but the feeling never lasts and instead we end up disillusioned.

It is the same pattern for all our needs if we look for their fulfillment in the wrong place. Inevitably we end up hurt and disappointed. The share market may collapse, our business may go bankrupt, our spouse may leave, our child may die, our creativity may dry up, our looks fade, and our sight diminish. Whatever we have put our faith in, if it is not in the right place, it will eventually fail us. It has to, because this is part of God's glorious plan.

WHERE ARE YOUR BASIC NEEDS MET?

If you are a Christian you may already know your real needs can only be truly met in a relationship with your Creator, who placed them within your heart. He designed you with your yearnings, your deepest desires, and deep, parched thirsts, and He alone is the source of the fountain that can quench them. He made you like this because, above all else, He loves you and longs for a deep meaningful relationship with you. Jesus says, "I am the way, the truth, and the life. No one comes to the Father except through Me" (John 14:6).

Only through a relationship with Jesus will God meet your deep needs. "I have come that [you] may have life, and that [you] may have it more abundantly" (John 10:10).

1. God gives you unconditional love.

> *Who shall separate [you] from the love of Christ? Shall tribulation, or distress, or persecution, or famine, or nakedness, or peril, or sword?...For I am persuaded that neither death nor life, nor angels nor principalities nor powers, nor things present nor things to come, nor height nor depth, nor any other created thing, shall be able to separate [you] from the love of God which is in Christ Jesus our Lord.* —ROMANS 8:35, 38–39

2. God gives you security.

> *The LORD by wisdom founded the earth; By understanding He established the heavens; By His knowledge the depths were broken up, And clouds drop down the dew. My son, let them not depart from your eyes...Then you will walk safely in your way, And your foot will not stumble. When you lie down, you will not be afraid; Yes, you will lie down and your sleep will be sweet. Do not be afraid of sudden terror, Nor of trouble from the wicked when it comes; For the LORD will be your confidence, And will keep your foot from being caught.* —PROVERBS 3:19–21, 23–26

> (SEE ALSO HEBREWS 4:16; PHILIPPIANS 1:6)

3. God gives your life significance.

> *For [you] are God's fellow workers; you are God's field, you are God's building.* —1 CORINTHIANS 3:9

Let a man so consider us, as servants of Christ and stewards of the mysteries of God.—1 CORINTHIANS 4:1

4. God has a meaningful purpose and plan for you.

"I know the plans I have for you," declares the LORD, "plans to prosper you and not to harm you, plans to give you hope and a future." —JEREMIAH 29:11, NIV

Sadly, even though you may know this is true in your head, for some reason it may not have reached your heart.

WHAT IS WRONG?

Sometimes the truth is hard to bring into experience and make a part of reality. Perhaps you recognize you have missed out on successfully making this transition of moving knowledge from your head into your heart. And instead you may have tasted elsewhere again and again and are stuck, gulping impulsively, compulsively, and obsessively from something that brings relief for only a brief moment and then slams you with guilt, shame, and hopelessness. And yet, even though you may know it's not working and never will, you seem powerless to stop yourself from being drawn back again and again, just in case it works this time. You think that if you try it slightly differently, or use more, you will make it. Maybe next time your deep thirst will be slaked.

Trapped in the cycle, chasing your backpack, adding weights with every circuit, you go around and around. For this is also where the addiction cycle can begin, and why it continues, as you try to alleviate emotional pain to:

Hide from shame

Drown loss

Forget the memory

Escape trauma

Ignore bad relationship

Avoid disappointment
Shortcut grief
Suppress dashed expectations

You can use almost anything in an attempt to alleviate this emotional pain: new relationships, sex, drugs, degrees, gambling, money, fetishes, food for comfort, or binging and then purging. *You are very inventive. You are made in your Father's image!* This deep emotional pain comes from missing out on having your very real needs met in an appropriate way. The lists of things people use to try and fill the gaps are endless.

Addiction is a weak attempt to have these real needs met now, in your timing. You don't want to wait! You like to do things your own way instead of seeking God's way. That is because of your rebellion and your demanding spirit. You don't like to wait for His timing because, in your eyes, it is too slow. Your attempts to meet your own needs your way are attempts to maintain control of your life on your terms. It may even be a sad attempt to maintain popularity with friends, submitting your weak will into the hands of others to keep them happy. As Gerald May says in his book *Will and Spirit*, "Addiction at its most fundamental level is a playing out of humanity's willful striving against the irrevocable mystery of consciousness and being. No where else do the issues of control and helplessness, mastery and surrender confront each other as brutally."[2]

THE RESULTS

In the process of maintaining an addiction, these cheap counterfeits, your way of meeting your perceived needs, eat away at your real will and deliver you into bondage. It doesn't take long. Before you even realize what is happening, your short bursts of behavior develop into a habit, and repeated habits develop into an addiction. Before you knew what was happening, you were trapped! Small, seemingly insignificant choices all bear fruit. You reap what you sow.

The satisfaction received at the beginning, the high that seemed to fulfill the burning desire within, is never repeated in its initial, full intensity. Addicts spend years trying to return to the intensity of their first hit by increasing the dose or the perversion a little more each time, but the high is never as good as it once was. It never will be. And by the time this is finally realized, if it ever is, the habit is firmly in place, the addiction taken hold, and the will to stop severely weakened. However, you still cling and grasp, hoping beyond all reason that it will work next time.

WHAT HAPPENS NEXT?

Does it end here? Of course not! Otherwise this book would not have been written! There is hope, but the sad reality is that addicts often lose sight of it. It is not found in trying harder. I'm sure if you are under bondage to addictive behavior you already know this, having tried many times to regain control and lead a healthy life, and it hasn't worked. It is not found in anything you can do on your own. Instead your hope is found in a Person. This Person is Jesus Christ. It is not found in your preconceived ideas of who Jesus is, but in who He really is and what He has done for you. Only He can truly fulfill your deep, real, and often haunting needs. Only He can set you free.

Paul said, "Now hope does not disappoint, because the love of God has been poured out in our hearts by the Holy Spirit who was given to us" (Rom. 5:5). This continually pouring love is the only fountain that will fill your real needs to the point of overflowing. You must find out how to drink from it. Paul says it has already been given to you, so what can you do to quench your thirst, what have you missed?

And here is the challenge—to kick addiction, you need to

find out who Jesus really is and what He offers you. You must start with the truth.

At the end of each chapter, a section called "Getting Real" is included to help you discover your real thoughts and feelings and identify where you stand right now. It is important to be very honest with yourself to make progress. Let's begin!

<u>GETTING REAL</u>

If you do not feel you have a personal relationship with your Creator and would like to ask Jesus Christ into your life and heart so He can fulfill your deepest needs, then pray this prayer:

Father in Heaven,

I believe You are the Creator of the universe. I believe You sent Your Son Jesus Christ into this world to die on the cross and rise again after three days to forgive my sins and set me free. I repent of all the things I have done wrong and ask You to forgive me. I ask Jesus to come into my heart. I surrender to You now and ask You to fulfill the basic needs in my life. In Jesus' name, Amen.

My name:

Am I a Christian?

If not, do I want to be?

Have I prayed the salvation prayer?

Do I have a problem with addictive behavior?

How long have I had this problem?

What have I tried to do about it?

Has it worked?

Chapter One

THE
TRUTH

*You shall know the truth,
and the truth shall make you free.*
—JOHN 8:32

Adam and Eve made a bad decision in the Garden of Eden. They chose to do their own thing instead of obeying God, and we have all suffered the consequences since.

Not only has their sin infected our minds, it has also changed our hearts into ones of rebellion. We all want our own way. We all want what we want right now—with cream on top!

The offshoot is that because God is so pure and holy, the sin we are now born with (thanks to Adam) has completely cut us off from relationship with Him. Next to His holiness and righteousness, every good thing we do looks like "filthy rags" (Isa. 64:6) in God's eyes. God looks down over all the earth and finds, "There is none who does good, No, not one" (Ps. 14:3). Trying harder won't help either. We just don't make the grade; we can't! The sinful disposition we inherited from our forefather Adam is part of who we are and no amount of good works or trying harder is going to take that away.

Yet our God is perfect and amazingly clever because He had a plan that blew the world apart (figuratively speaking). Because man could never get it right in his own strength, God sent His perfect and only Son, Jesus Christ, down to Earth to do the job for us. That's why Jesus was born of a virgin in a manger, and it's why He died—to deal with the part of us that can never get it right with God.

Jesus died on the cross to restore your relationship with your Father and to fulfill all your basic needs. Jesus died to pay the price for your sins so that you can be set free. He came "to preach the gospel to the poor…to heal the broken-hearted, To proclaim liberty to the captives And recovery of sight to the blind, To set at liberty those who are oppressed" (Luke 4:18).

As you come to understand more of what He has done for you, you will begin to see the truth. As your eyes are opened further, your understanding is enlightened. We will look at this freedom and what God has to offer in the next chapter, but for now let's look more deeply at the truth, for this is the first step towards freedom.

Before going on, prepare yourself by praying this simple prayer:

Lord Jesus,
Please open my eyes and my understanding so that I may see Your truth. Amen.

GOD IS NUMBER ONE

Who is your mighty Creator, your Father in heaven?

Who is like You, O LORD?…glorious in holiness, Fearful in praises, doing wonders? —EXODUS 15:11

The LORD, the LORD God, merciful and gracious, longsuffering, and abounding in goodness and truth, keeping mercy for thousands, forgiving iniquity and transgression and sin, by no means clearing the guilty. —EXODUS 34:6–7

He is the Rock, His work is perfect; For all His ways are justice. A God of truth and without injustice; Righteous and upright is He. —DEUTERONOMY 32:4

God is love. —1 JOHN 4:8

Our God is in heaven; He does whatever He pleases. —PSALM 115:3

For God so loved the world that He gave His only begotten Son, that whoever believes in Him should not perish but have everlasting life. —JOHN 3:16

If you love Me, keep My commandments. —JOHN 14:15

Because God created the whole universe, at the end of all arguments, thoughts, and meanderings of the mind, there is one simple fact—it's all about Him! And He wants to have a relationship with you. People often try to make it complicated, but God's ways are very simple. He asks you to come like a little child. "Unless you are converted and become as little children, you will by no means enter the kingdom of heaven" (Matt. 18:3). What are little children like? They ask for what they want. They have thousands of questions. Some of the answers are far too difficult for them to understand, but they ask anyway. They always believe the best, believing their parents are trustworthy and honest, even if they don't live up to these huge expectations. However, your Father in heaven does, even if you don't understand the way He goes about it sometimes.

Your Father in heaven is perfect; not only in His character, His holiness, knowledge, love, goodness, mercy, kindness, patience, faithfulness, and wisdom, but also in everything He does, including His judgments. He is far above all you can imagine. He is a mighty, mysterious God and yet He wants you to know Him:

> *"Let not the wise man glory in his wisdom, Let not the mighty man glory in his might, Nor let the rich man glory in his riches; But let him who glories glory in this, That he understands and knows Me, That I am the LORD, exercising lovingkindness, judgment, and righteousness in the earth. For in these I delight," says the LORD.*
> —JEREMIAH 9:23–24

It's amazing to think the Creator of the universe desires you to know Him in such depth. It is so important to Him that He has placed this as the wellspring for all you experience in life both now and into eternity. "And this is eternal life, that they may know You, the only true God, and Jesus Christ whom You have sent" (John 17:3).

The task of getting to know God is awe inspiring from wherever you stand. It is almost beyond understanding. In fact it would be, except that God has made provision to help you. Jesus made it clear He does not expect you to get to know Him, follow Him, and obey Him in your own strength. He promises, "I will pray the Father, and He will give you another Helper, that He may abide with you forever—the Spirit of truth, whom the world cannot receive, because it neither sees Him nor knows Him; but you know Him, for He dwells with you and will be in you" (John 14:16–17).

The Holy Spirit has been given to you, living inside you, to lead you into all truth. "When He, the Spirit of truth, has come, He will guide you into all truth; for He will not speak on His own authority, but whatever He hears He will speak; and He will tell you things to come" (John 16:13).

One of the main works of the Spirit is to glorify Jesus Christ and He does this for an amazing reason. The truth is not just ideas, doctrines, or suggestions. The truth is a Person. It is Jesus Christ Himself. Remember Jesus said, "I am the way, the truth, and the life. No one comes to the Father except through Me" (John 14:6).

It takes a lifetime to get to know God more. In fact it will take eternity—He is so mysterious and amazing—but you can start right now if you choose to!

LOOKING AT YOU

Thanks to what Jesus has already done on the cross, if you have accepted Him as your Lord and Savior, God no longer sees you as a sinner. Instead He sees you as a saint. Isn't it time you started to see yourself this way?

God does not see you as an addict, so stop calling yourself one. He sees you as His child—a prince or princess in His kingdom, an heir to His throne. You belong to your Father in heaven. He bought you for a huge price. It cost Him the life of His only Son and He calls you to live as His heir, a child of worth, honor, and dignity. You are special in God's eyes. He made you completely unique. There is no one in the whole earth like you, no one with your fingerprints, your passions, or your personality. He cares about every detail in your life and has a special plan that only you can fulfill (see Jer. 29:11). He even told you how to discover this plan. "Then you will call upon Me and go and pray to Me, and I will listen to you. And you will seek Me and find Me, when you search for Me with all your heart" (Jer. 29:12–13). You need to search with all your heart, not just part of it! Amazingly, the scripture doesn't end here either. God tells you the result. "I will be found by you, says the LORD, and I will bring you back from your captivity" (Jer. 29:14).

Addiction is captivity. God has something so much better for you that stretches into your future for eternity. It is a plan far more wonderful than anything you can ever imagine, because it is your perfect Father in heaven's plan.

Before you can begin to see the beauty of God's plan for you, you may need to take your eyes off yourself and look at Him. We all do! And it's hard. For a moment you need to accept yourself for who you are right now. Not your "improved," false, face-lifted advertisement of yourself, but right now, just as you are, this moment. And with this view in mind, however pathetic, painful, or unbelievable the sight may be in all its rawness, take it, fall in love with it, and then look toward God.

You may wonder what you could possibly love about yourself when you think of your brokenness. Perhaps it is your love of nature, your sense of humor, your strong legs, or even your cute ears! However, above all else, even if you feel there is nothing else, you can love yourself because you are made in God's image! "Let Us make man in Our image, according to Our likeness" (Gen. 1:26).

Self-acceptance is the place where you turn away from your self-centeredness, and with your eyes and every other part of you, look outward towards everything else in creation. It is a difficult place to reach if you are still unsure of who you are and are searching for your identity. It is a place that affects each of us until we come to acknowledge who we really are in our incompleteness and then bring this before God to soak in His love and acceptance and receive His help. Your identity is ultimately in Him. And so is your wholeness. Yet sometimes this seems so difficult to grasp.

Imagine you are a king, and as you stride through your city streets you spy a young boy lying in the gutter. No one seems to notice him, but you tell your chauffeur to pick him up and take him home. You legally adopt him into your family, feed him, clothe him, let him live in your house, use your entertainment center, and even give him an unlimited credit card facility. One day, while on your way to an international leader's convention, you see the boy foraging in a garbage can looking for something to eat? How would you feel, after all you have done for him and having loved him so dearly?

Sit with this feeling for a moment, because this is how God feels when you refuse to accept how much He loves you and all He offers, and instead choose to ferret around waste lands sipping from broken cisterns that will never satisfy your needs and desires. God is deeply grieved by your sin. When He looked down on all the wickedness in the earth at the time of Noah, the Bible says, "He was grieved in His heart" (Gen. 6:6) This is how God feels about you when you don't accept what He has done for you.

The boy did not understand what he had been given. He didn't understand he no longer had to live the way he had lived in the past. He had entered into a new world, a new kingdom, a place that was filled with wonderful surprises, with things he had never seen before, things he had never known existed. And new things can seem strange at first. Sometimes it takes a while to adjust.

Change can be difficult. It's rarely easy! But remember:

> *What the caterpillar calls the end of the*
> *world the master calls a butterfly.*[1]
> **—RICHARD BACH**

It can help to understand your surroundings a little better. We will look inside this new kingdom in the next chapter. It is a place of great treasure.

Jesus says the "kingdom of heaven is like a merchant seeking beautiful pearls, who, when he had found one pearl of great price, went and sold all that he had and bought it" (Matt. 13:45–46). It is of such value that when you understand more of what it has to offer, nothing else in the world will compare with your appreciation of it. Derek Prince also points to another meaning of this verse, which illustrates God's extravagant love for you. Not only can you be seen as the merchant, giving up all you have to purchase the kingdom, but Jesus is also the merchant and you are the pearl. When He knew you, He gave up all He had to bring you into His family and adopt you as His child. You are this special in His eyes.

GETTING REAL

Do I know who God really is?

How can I find out more?

Do I regularly read my Bible? If not, will I start today?

Do I speak with Him every day? If not, will I start now?

Do I understand who I am in God's eyes?

Do I see myself as a saint or a sinner?

If I really understood that I am a prince or princess in God's family, what would I do differently?

What small steps can I take to move in this direction?

What do I know about God's kingdom?

Am I walking in it?

Chapter Two

THE KINGDOM OF GOD:
WHAT DOES HE OFFER?

*Do not fear, little flock, for it is your
Father's good pleasure to give you
the kingdom.* —LUKE 12:32

In Romans 14:17 we are told, "the kingdom of God is not eating and drinking, but righteousness and peace and joy in the Holy Spirit." When you are born again into this kingdom, life changes. Facts change!

When you accept Jesus Christ as your Savior:

1. You are adopted as His son or daughter.

> *He chose us…having predestined us to adoption as sons by Jesus Christ…according to the good pleasure of His will.* —EPHESIANS 1:4–5

2. You become an heir to everything He has.

> *You received the Spirit of adoption by whom we cry out, "Abba, Father."…and if children, then heirs—heirs of God and joint heirs with Christ.* —ROMANS 8:15, 17

3. You have the indwelling Holy Spirit to assist you.

The Holy Spirit, whom the Father will send in My name, He will teach you all things. —JOHN 14:26

4. You have the right to come before God's throne and ask for what you need.

Let us therefore come boldly to the throne of grace, that we may obtain mercy and find grace to help in time of need. —HEBREWS 4:16

5. You have good works that God has already prepared in advance for you to do.

We are…created…for good works, which God prepared beforehand that we should walk in them. —EPHESIANS 2:10

6. You have provision for everything and anything God asks you to do.

And my God shall supply all your need according to His riches in glory by Christ Jesus. —PHILIPPIANS 4:19

7. You have supernatural protection.

The God of Israel will be your rear guard. —ISAIAH 52:12

He is a shield to all who trust in Him. —2 SAMUEL 22:31

8. You have hope.

Now hope does not disappoint, because the love of God has been poured out in our hearts by the Holy Spirit who was given to us. —ROMANS 5:5

9. You are set free.

Therefore if the Son makes you free, you shall be free indeed. —JOHN 8:36

What does He mean by *free*? Let's pause and get real for a moment:

ARE YOU FREE?

If you have a problem with addictive behavior, you're unlikely to feel free. Your repetitive, addictive behavior is binding you to your old life—to the "old man." It is trapping you to "broken cisterns" that can never quench your very real thirst.

Deep down you probably know this. You feel it at the deepest level of your heart and if you have any desire to be a disciple of Christ you will also feel the deep shame and helplessness that comes with this knowledge. But remember, this is a good thing. It puts you in the right relationship with God, understanding that He is your Creator and you are the creature. Jesus says, "Without Me you can do nothing" (John 15:5). From this stance of being the creature, you know what He is talking about. You may have tried to do it on your own; you may have tried to change and you have failed. Jesus is right. Without Him you can do nothing.

Like the young boy who chose to go back to the garbage can, sometimes without fully understanding why, you may have chosen to wallow in your defeat. Sometimes we reject good ideas and choices because we don't understand them.

Let's look more closely at the freedom God offers in your relationship with Him. This freedom is not a license to do whatever you please.

All True Freedom Requires Responsibility

God has set guidelines in place for your own good. He knows the mess you can make if you are left to yourself. Imagine a game of football without any rules. It would be utter chaos. And this is how your life will end up if you fail to do things God's way. God's freedom does set you free. It does it in such a way that you can experience the abundance real life has to offer.

We Are Given Freedom from Some Things and Freedom for Other Things.

As a child of God you have:

1. **Freedom from the control of others**
   Jesus says:

   Follow Me, and let the dead bury their own dead.
   —MATTHEW 8:22

2. **Freedom to control yourself**

   But the fruit of the Spirit is…self-control.
   —GALATIANS 5:23

3. **Freedom to know the truth**

   If you abide in My word…you shall know the truth, and the truth shall make you free. —JOHN 8:31–32

4. **Freedom to be you in the fullness God intended**

   I have come that [you] may have life, and that [you] may have it more abundantly. —JOHN 10:10

5. Freedom from your past

When you come in repentance God has *"forgiven you all trespasses, having wiped out the handwriting of requirements that was against us, which was contrary to us. And He has taken it out of the way, having nailed it to the cross"* (Col. 2:13–14).

6. Freedom from want

He will *"supply all your need according to His riches in glory by Christ Jesus"* (Phil. 4:19). This not only means material requirements like food and clothing, but also all your needs for unconditional love, security, significance, strength, energy, health, internal peace, talents, abilities, and even joy. It includes everything you will ever need to fulfill His will in your life.

7. Freedom from worry

"Therefore do not worry, saying, 'What shall we eat?' or 'What shall we drink?' or 'What shall we wear?'… For your heavenly Father knows that you need all these things. But seek first the kingdom of God and His righteousness, and all these things shall be added to you" (Matt. 6:31–33). God already knows the plan. He knows what you need to fulfill it, so you can leave the worry to Him!

8. Freedom from fear

"God has not given us a spirit of fear, but of power and of love and of a sound mind" (2 Tim. 1:7). Because He knows everything and is all powerful, nothing can happen to you that has not already passed through His hand and that He will not equip you to handle even though it may seem devastating at the time.

9. Freedom from debt

By following the principles in Scripture (especially Proverbs) you can come to the place where you, *"Owe no one anything except to love one another"* (Rom. 13:8). Many of your financial problems may come from greed and mismanagement. You want what you want now and are not prepared to wait until you can afford it!

10. Freedom to succeed

God gives particular gifts and abilities to help complete tasks He has given. When the Israelites built the tabernacle, God told Moses, *"I have put wisdom in the hearts of all the gifted artisans, that they may make all that I have commanded you"* (Exod. 31:6). God will equip you but you must do your part of maintaining and practicing your skills.

11. Freedom to love and experience real joy

"If you keep My commandments, you will abide in My love…that My joy may remain in you, and that your joy may be full. This is My commandment, that you love one another as I have loved you" (John 15:10–12). Real joy is found in being in the center of God's will glorifying Him. Love and joy are both fruits of the Spirit (see Gal. 5:22).

12. Freedom to enjoy your salvation

"For by grace you have been saved through faith, and that not of yourselves; it is the gift of God" (Eph. 2:8) *"The Son gives life to whom He will"* (John 5:21). It's time to enjoy this wonderful gift of life.

13. Freedom to enjoy eternal life

"And this is the testimony: that God has given us eternal life, and this life is in His Son" (1 John 5:11). You no lon-

ger need to fear death. For Christians it is a transition experience into the fullness of God's kingdom.

14. Freedom from bondage to sin

"Whoever commits sin is a slave of sin… if the Son makes you free, you shall be free indeed" (John 8:34–36). We will look at this in more depth in a later chapter. But for now it is important to remember:

Addictive behavior is sin—it is seeking to meet a need outside God's provision. It is the sin of idolatry.

The benefits and freedom provided in God's kingdom are available to you now. It is God's pleasure to give them to you. You do not need to wait until you go to heaven. It is time to walk through the door!

GETTING REAL

Are you free?

Can you identify areas where you are not free?
What are they?

Do you acknowledge addictive behavior as sin?
If not, why not?

What can you do about it?

Are you ready to walk in His kingdom?

Chapter Three

REPENTANCE

*It is well for people who think, to change
their minds occasionally in order to keep
them clean.[1] —LUTHER BURBANK*

Addictive behavior is the sin of idolatry. It also encompasses the sin of disobedience and may include many other sins such as sexual sin, gluttony, and lying. Sin is sin in God's eyes. We are told there are some sins that deserve greater punishment than others (see John 19:11), but the end result of all sin is the same—death. "The wages of sin is death" (Rom. 6:23). It's no good relying on God's goodness to let you off the hook. He says He will "by no means [clear] the guilty" (Exod. 34:7). And that means you, if you are still involved in addictive behavior. If God lets anyone off the hook because they are a nice person, He would no longer be a good God because He would be condoning evil. And God is so good and so holy He will never do that.

God has made His conditions very clear.

*I have set before you today life and good, death and evil,
in that I command you today to love the LORD your God,
to walk in His ways, and to keep His commandments, His
statutes, and His judgments, that you may live and multi-*

ply; and the LORD your God will bless you…But if your heart turns away so that you do not hear, and are drawn away, and worship other gods and serve them, I announce to you today that you shall surely perish…I have set before you life and death; blessing and cursing; therefore choose life, that both you and your descendants may live.
—DEUTERONOMY 30:15–19

Even though this majestic challenge was given in Old Testament days, God's ways have not changed. The wages of sin are still death (Rom. 6:23). Death is separation from God and all He represents. If you choose death it means your destiny will involve separation from all truth, light, goodness, joy, and love if you do not restore your relationship with Him.

There is only one way to restore your relationship with God—you need to trust in the work Jesus has already done on the cross and repent.

The key issue here is to trust in the work Jesus has already completed on the cross. We will examine this in the next chapter. Out of this trust flows repentance as you begin to see how you have hurt God in not believing Him and accepting what He has done for you. You need to realize the work is complete and finished, and walk in it. Then repentance makes sense.

Repentance means turning one hundred eighty degrees away from sin and asking God to forgive you. It requires a change of heart, mind, and will. It involves the whole person and needs to result in action.

We see this in the parable of the prodigal son. He asked for his inheritance, went to a foreign land, and squandered everything on high living, wine, women, and perhaps an occasional song. He lost it all and found himself working in a pig sty, eating worse food than the pigs. While he was there, it occurred to him his father's servants ate better food than he did. He "came to himself." This was his change of mind. His thinking changed. He was tired of feeding pigs and smelling like them and remembered the wholesome life he left behind. He realized the state of his own heart, his self-centeredness and sinfulness, and confessed, "I have sinned" (Luke 15:18). And he chose a new direction one hundred and eighty degrees away from where he was and put this decision into action. He actually had to do something. He walked home. "I will arise and go to my father" (Luke 15:18). The son had no idea what response he would receive when he arrived home, but regardless of the outcome he was determined to try and make things right. His money was gone, he couldn't get that back, but perhaps the important relationships in his life could be salvaged.

The young man could have decided to change his life, to give up his bad habits, and turn over a new leaf, but this is not repentance. True repentance results in "repentance toward God and faith toward our Lord Jesus Christ" (Acts 20:21). This faith believes that Christ died for your sins, was buried, and rose from the dead to give you newness of life (see 1 Cor. 15:3–4). It believes He became sin for you, paying the price for you, so that He can dwell within you and live His life through you. It is not about you trying harder to please Him. He does the living—you need to let Him live through you by understanding what He has done, realizing this truth, and walking in that realization.

REAL REPENTANCE BEARS FRUIT

Real repentance leads to a life of righteousness involving a complete turning away from unrighteousness, in humility allowing God to live in you, yielding to Him, depending on Him to help maintain your position. And it leads toward a deeply satisfying and truly renewed relationship with God, seeking His kingdom and ways. Anything less is not the real thing and God is all about being real.

You will discover as you move toward the depths of repentance that there are many other sins that may seem insignificant at first, which have led up to major sin in your life. All these seemingly smaller sins need to be repented of also.

Paul tells us what real repentance looks like:

> *What diligence it produced in you, what clearing of your-selves, what indignation, what fear, what vehement desire, what zeal, what vindication!* —2 CORINTHIANS 7:11

The Amplified Bible makes the process even clearer. It points to:

An eagerness and earnest care to explain and clear yourself

Indignation at sin

Alarm

Yearning and zeal to do justice to all concerned

A readiness to give punishment to the offender

This is no half-baked pity party. This is the real thing. It is a heartfelt urgency and determination to put things right. But how do you get there?

THE WAY TO GENUINE REPENTANCE

There are two kinds of sorrow recorded in Scripture: worldly sorrow and godly sorrow. Worldly sorrow ends in a "pity party" and is more concerned with being sorry for getting caught! "The sorrow of the world produces death" (2 Cor. 7:10). However, Paul tells us "Godly sorrow produces repentance leading to salvation, not to be regretted" (2 Cor. 7:10).

It is not wise to think you can enter into this godly sorrow that leads to repentance anytime you wish. You may think you'll continue in your sin for a while longer until you feel like changing, or have more money, or God changes your circumstances, but genuine repentance is a gift and needs to be received when it is given. "Him [Jesus] God has exalted to His right hand to be Prince and Savior, to give repentance to Israel and forgiveness of sins" (Acts 5:31). You never know when it will be offered again. The disciples were not sure. When Paul was advising believers on how to treat those who were in opposition, he said, "in humility correcting those who are in opposition, *if God perhaps will grant them repentance,* so that they may know the truth, and that they may come to their senses and escape the snare of the devil, having been taken captive by him to do his will" (2 Tim. 2:25–26, emphasis added). Paul wasn't sure of God's response.

If you feel any inclination to repent, do it now, believing God has led you to this window of opportunity for restoring your relationship with Him. Repentance is not something you can choose whenever you want, expect as a right, or arrogantly despise. It is a very special, precious opportunity to connect again with your Father's heart and take your place under the shadow of His wings in His protection and care. When the window appears, take it.

Unfortunately, if you refuse, you will change. Your heart will harden and sadly, perhaps eventually, you will never even want to journey back toward God again. Every choice you make brings change and every change is a move toward God and what He offers, your salvation, or a move away from Him. Paul says that people who refuse to acknowledge God and the work He is doing in their lives become "futile in their thoughts, and their foolish hearts were darkened" (Rom. 1:21). As a result, "as they did not like to retain God in their knowledge, God gave them over to a debased mind, to do those things which are not fitting" (Rom. 1:28). Who knows when or even if the window of repentance will be offered again!

If you feel the need and desire to repent, pray this prayer:

Dear Lord,

I have fallen short of Your glory and the plans You have for my life. I repent now of _______________ (name every sin that comes to mind).

If there is anything else, Lord, please let the Holy Spirit convict me and bring it to mind.

(Now repent by name of these things.)

Lord, I thank You for Your wonderful forgiveness and pray that You will guide and help me every moment, every step of the way, so that I may show the fruits of repentance and glorify Your name.

Thank You in Jesus' name. Amen.

> *If we confess our sins, He is faithful and just to forgive us our sins and to cleanse us from all unrighteousness.*
> —1 JOHN 1:9

You are forgiven because God always keeps His word.

What can you expect as a result of your repentance? Oswald Chambers says, "Repentance does not bring a sense of sin, but a sense of unutterable unworthiness. When I repent, I realize that I am utterly helpless; I know all through me that I am not worthy even to bear His shoes. Have I repented like that? Or is there a lingering suggestion of standing up by myself? The reason God cannot come into my life is because I am not through into repentance."[2] He suggests that if you have not entered into victory in your life it is because you have not truly entered into the depths of repentance.

However, if you have, or are in the process of entering into this place, let's discover how you can stay cleansed from all unrighteousness.

<u>GETTING REAL</u>

Do I need to pray the prayer of repentance?

Have I done it? If not, why not?

What am I waiting for?

Will waiting help?

If I have and it hasn't "stuck" or "worked," what kind of sorrow am I displaying?

What is missing?

Chapter Four

PUTTING OFF THE OLD AND PUTTING ON THE NEW

Seek those things which are above, where
Christ is, sitting at the right hand of God.
—COLOSSIANS 3:1

When you sin, you "put on the old man" by living in the fallen world in the same manner unbelievers do. Psalm 109:18 explains, "As he clothed himself with cursing as with his garment, So let it enter his body like water, And like oil into his bones." The sin became part of him. When you choose to sin it seeps through your whole being and affects you in far greater ways than you imagine. It is a frightening thing to realize how much willful sin can change you. We have already read that God eventually gives you over to a "debased mind."

In contrast Leanne Payne explains what happens when you "put on the new man." "The moment we put on Christ and the transient good, our real, new self starts clamoring at the bars of any foul thing that imprisons it. It then breaks those bars and bursts through to truth and substantive reality; it rises to connect with a holy presence."[1] In the same way sin affects you adversely, doing the right thing affects your whole being in a positive way.

The question is, How can you "put on the new man"? As you already know, trying harder doesn't work. Paul describes the problem of making it a reality in his experience. "For I know that in me (that is, in my flesh) nothing good dwells; for to will is present with me, but how to perform what is good I do not find. For the good that I will to do, I do not do; but the evil I will not to do, that I practice" (Rom. 7:18–19). In other words he wanted to do what was right but kept doing what he knew was wrong. He wasn't living up to his own standard of integrity. Everyone suffering under the bondage of addictive behavior will identify with this dilemma.

However, the truth is even more devastating when it sinks deeply into your soul. Do you realize that even your best is nowhere near God's standard? Everything you do is worthless in His eyes. In your own strength you are totally incapable of ever achieving God's will, no matter how much effort you put into it. As Watchman Nee says, "My failure in regard to God's will makes my body a body of death…In regard to all that is wicked, worldly and Satanic I am, in my nature, wholly positive; but in regard to all that pertains to holiness and heaven and God I am wholly negative."[2]

Your only hope lies in understanding what Christ achieved in dying on the cross. You already know He dealt with your daily sins so that when you repent, you are forgiven for what you do wrong, but like many Christians, you may not understand He also dealt with your sinful disposition that was inherited from Adam when he committed the original sin, and He dealt with your natural man or "flesh." Consequently you may not yet have entered into the fullness of the work Jesus completed on the cross.

The disciple John says, "If we confess our sins, He is faithful and just to forgive us our sins and to cleanse us from all unrighteousness" (1 John 1:9). The first part of this verse deals with the first part of the work Jesus accomplished, forgiving your daily sins. The second part deals with your sinful disposition that was inherited from Adam, and your flesh, saying He will "cleanse us from all unrighteousness." Amazingly, just as the first part is a work already completed because Jesus has already died and risen again, so the second part of the verse is also a completed work. It needs to be worked out in your life only in the sense that you must enter into what has already been done. You need to receive it by faith to walk into these truths with the help of the Holy Spirit, by walking in the Spirit. It is almost like discovering and walking into new rooms in the kingdom of God, rooms that have been there all along but for some reason you have continually walked past them in your ignorance or misunderstanding. Perhaps you thought that such places do not exist or that if they do they are for other people and not you, or perhaps that you have to build the rooms yourself, in your own strength, using your own will power.

If you are under the bondage of addictive behavior you will already know you can't build these rooms with your own strength. These rooms, like every other place in the kingdom of God, are already available to you, they are there for the using. They are already yours as a right because you are an heir to all Jesus has given you. You are a son or daughter of the King of kings and everything He has is available to you. And like all of God's gifts they are received by faith.

Jesus made these rooms available to you because of His work. He opened the way for you to be reconciled to God on an intimate basis. And because God is a holy and righteous God, Jesus opened the way for you to thoroughly change your mind, will, and emotions as you accept the work He has already completed so that you can commune with your Holy Father. Jesus did this for everyone who will commit their lives to Him. He took the weight of the world's sin on His shoulders to accomplish this. Imagine the pain, the torture He endured to take this weight in your place, the weight of the entire world's sin from beginning to end so that you might be set free to change, set free from fear, set free to love, and set free to live in His glorious freedom.

If you are a Christian you are not unfamiliar with this concept. To even become a Christian you needed to die to your old life and literally give your life to Christ, trusting Him to rebuild you in His image. This is symbolized through water baptism. "Therefore we were buried with Him through baptism into death, that just as Christ was raised from the dead by the glory of the Father, even so we also should walk in newness of life" (Rom. 6:4). New life starts with a death. Think again of the butterfly. What the caterpillar calls death, the butterfly calls birth into a new life. There is always a death that precedes new life.

Paul goes on to explain that in this symbolic transaction "our old man was crucified with Him, that the body of sin might be done away with, that we should no longer be slaves of sin. For he who has died has been freed from sin" (Rom. 6:6–7). This "body of sin" refers to your sinful disposition inherited from Adam. Christ died on the cross to gain victory over this disposition so that it no longer controls you. His death secured the victory. Notice Paul uses the past tense—"was crucified." The victory has already been won.

This sounds great. Jesus has done the work. And yet how can this truth be grasped to become a reality in daily life? How does it work in practice?

Paul also discovered how to join the theory with reality. He says to "reckon [yourself] to be dead indeed to sin, but alive to God in Christ Jesus our Lord" (Rom. 6:11). To reckon means to accept something as certain.[3] It is a matter of believing to receive, of realizing the simple truths of what Jesus has already done for you. What are you supposed to reckon? What do you need to believe? Or more to the point, whom do you need to believe? Seeing his inability to achieve this on his own, Paul cries out "O wretched man that I am! Who will deliver me from this body of death?" And he gives the answer. "I thank

God—through Jesus Christ our Lord!" (Rom. 7:24–25). You need to believe in Christ for this, in the same way you believed for your salvation. You need to believe that your sinful disposition has actually already died with Christ on the cross and you no longer have to live in bondage to it. You are set free by what Christ has already done for you. The work is completed! It is a matter of believing to receive, of realizing the simple truth of what Jesus has already done.

This process of believing and learning to receive can be difficult. The whole process needs to start with a death, and death is never pleasant. But think of the comparison between the life of the caterpillar and the life of a butterfly. The caterpillar has to crawl painstakingly from leaf to leaf and branch to branch always watching over its shoulder and around its many legs to see who might be trying to devour it. The butterfly is free to soar through the air from one beautiful flower to the next, free to enjoy all the world has to offer. Who would you rather be?

Paul says, "he who has died has been freed from sin…For sin shall not have dominion over you, for you are not under law but under grace" (Rom. 6:7, 14). We will look more closely at God's grace in a later chapter to understand more clearly how this works, but for now we will concentrate on the freedom you already have. Your thinking needs to change to accommodate this truth. Your mind needs to be renewed.

Paul says:

> *The truth is in Jesus: that you put off, concerning your former conduct, the old man which grows corrupt according to the deceitful lusts, and be renewed in the spirit of your mind, and that you put on the new man which was created according to God, in true righteousness and holiness.*
> —EPHESIANS 4:21–24

You need to seek God and ask Him to make this real to you. It is found in Romans 6–8. You need a personal revelation from God. Study it and pray over it until it becomes your own revelation.

Your "flesh" that place in you that wants to do its own thing but is now dead to the bondage of sin, is the other part that can also want to take control. It is the natural man, the "self" or "soul" with all its desires, hopes, and dreams. Your motivation may even be to try harder to please God. Yet this is not God's plan for you and Christ also dealt with this on the cross. Galatians 2:20 says, "I have been crucified with Christ; it is no longer I who live, but Christ lives in me; and the life which I now live in the flesh I live by faith in the Son of God, who loved me and gave Himself for me." This "I" or "flesh" has also died on the cross, making it possible to walk with God in righteousness, with the Holy Spirit's help. And this truth must also be believed and received to become a reality in your life.

You may wonder exactly what you are to put off and put on in your new life. Paul tells you in Colossians 3:8–15.

> *Put off all these: anger, wrath, malice, blasphemy, filthy language out of your mouth. Do not lie to one another, since you have put off the old man with his deeds, and have put on the new man who is renewed in knowledge…put on tender mercies, kindness, humility, meekness, long-suffering; bearing with one another, and forgiving one another, if anyone has a complaint against another; even as Christ forgave you, so you also must do. But above all these things put on love, which is the bond of perfection. And let the peace of God rule in your hearts, to which also you were called in one body; and be thankful.*

Your new purpose in life, by entering into these rooms in the kingdom of God, is to "serve in the newness of the Spirit" (Rom. 7:6). Paul declares, "to be carnally minded is death, but to be spiritually minded is life and peace" (Rom. 8:6).

Living in the Spirit and walking in the Spirit means that you trust in the Spirit to do in you what you cannot do in your own strength. It means a moment-by-moment dependence on the Spirit to lead and guide you. Watchmen Nee describes it well. "It is not a case of trying but of trusting; not of struggling but of resting in Him."[4] You allow Christ to live out His life inside and through you, but it does not happen through your efforts.

This new place and way of being is only found in dependence, trust, and obedience. Looking ahead the task may seem daunting, but it is like changing your clothes. Pull the old, filthy, ragged jersey off over your head, and the ripped shirt, then put on the new, clean suit of clothes God has given you. Yes, the crusty old clothes were comforting, and yes, the new suit may seem a little stiff at first, but you are commanded to do this by God who knows and wants what is best for you in the long run. Can you obey for this first minute? For this is all you need to do. Now can you obey for this next minute? Of course you can. And this is all you are ever required to do—to obey minute by minute, hour by hour, one day at a time.

The revelation of these truths of the work Jesus has already completed needs to sink deeply into your spirit, for revelation always precedes growth of faith and the out-working of experience in your life. Dwell in these truths, dare to wander into these rooms in the kingdom of God, and taste and see that they are good.

GETTING REAL

Have I been trying to use my own self-control and will to stop my addictive behavior?

Has it worked?

Why not?

What do I need to understand to enter into all Christ has done for me?

Are these new concepts for me?

What do these new rooms in God's kingdom look and feel like to me?

Stay in these rooms and explore them for a moment.

Chapter Five

RENEWING THE MIND:
ADDICTIVE THINKING

For as he thinks in his heart, so is he.
—PROVERBS 23:7

Scripture says to "be transformed by the renewing of your mind, that you may prove what is that good and acceptable and perfect will of God" (Rom. 12:2). After years of incorrect and addictive thinking, renewing your mind can be a formidable task! But with God's help "all things are possible" (Matt. 19:26).

Let's look at some of the unhealthy ways of thinking that have trapped you into addictive behavior, and replace them with the truth. Many of these patterns of thinking are unconscious mechanisms. They come from a distorted self-image, a failure of seeing who you are in your relationship with God. Because they are unconscious, you will usually need someone else to point them out to you.

The unconscious, distorted self's purpose behind addictive thinking is to allow you to continue in your destructive behavior. Addictive thinking is different from logical thinking in that it does not reach a conclusion based on the evidence or the facts in a situation, but instead bases its conclusion on lies, formulated to help justify your behavior.

Addictive thinking reflects your inability to make wise, consistently healthy decisions about yourself. It reflects an inability to use your "will" effectively in this particular area of your life, although thinking may be normal in all other areas of life.

Many of the quirks of addictive thinking are set up as defenses against anxiety, depression, fear of rejection, isolation, despair, and even grief. Some addictive thinkers struggle to feel "normal" at all except when they are "acting out" their addictive behavior or are under the influence of drugs or alcohol.

Addictive thinking is a twisted way to avoid an awareness you have decided is unacceptable. This decision may be at a subconscious level. You may not be fully aware you have even made the choice. The reasons for setting up these defense mechanisms may be as varied as individuals, but nevertheless at their foundation is always a refusal to face the truth because it is painful.

Honesty is essential in any effort to overcome all forms of addictive thinking. Let's now look at some of these mechanisms and see how they can be replaced with the truth.

Denial

This is when you fail to see the truth, your responsibility, or that you even have a problem. Denial works. You may be so good at it that you even believe you are telling the truth. The force behind denial is a strong resistance to change. And instead of facing the truth and reality in your life and changing yourself, all your efforts may be focused on trying to change others or your environment.

The truth

King David says of God, "You desire truth in the inward parts, And in the hidden part You will make me to know wisdom" (Ps. 51:6). God wants you to face truth and He will help you to do so if you ask Him. He has given you the Holy Spirit for this purpose (see John 16:13).

Rationalization

You may be very good at giving "good" reasons instead of true reasons. This diverts everyone's attention away from the truth and is another way to avoid making changes that need to be made in your life. You can become so good at rationalization that you are unaware you are doing it, and so good that everyone else believes you.

The truth

"And you shall know the truth, and the truth shall make you free" (John 8:32). It is only when you stop making excuses and coming up with "good" reasons that you are in a position where God can help you become free. Make a decision today to stop lying, for anything short of the truth is a lie.

Projection

Projection is when you blame everyone else for your problems instead of taking responsibility yourself. It always seems so reasonable, but in the end you are responsible not only for your behavior but also your feelings.

The truth

"Every one shall die for his own iniquity" (Jer. 31:30). "For the wages of sin is death" (Rom. 6:23). Face the truth of your sin and inadequacies and come to repentance where necessary. This restores your relationship with God and puts you in a position to receive His direction and guidance.

Anger

Anger is a normal, healthy emotion when it is used in the right way. It has been given to help preserve social order and propel you into action when you see injustice. Addictive thinkers have trouble keeping their anger in perspective and learning how to deal with it in a healthy way. You may have extremes of emotions because you take things so personally. This is because you are still very self-centered. Subsequently you may experience rage over seemingly small matters. Your perceptions are distorted and therefore your emotional responses will also be distorted.

The truth

"'Be angry, and do not sin': do not let the sun go down on your wrath, nor give place to the devil" (Eph. 4:26–27). Anger itself is not a sin, but it can become one if used in the wrong way. God wants you to see the truth and place responsibility where it belongs. If it belongs to someone else you may need to confront them. If it belongs to you, you will need to take responsibility and deal with it appropriately. You may need the help of a counselor to do this.

False guilt and shame

Real guilt can be dealt with through repentance. However, false guilt is when you take on other people's guilt as though it were yours, or when you take on responsibility for things that are not your responsibility. False guilt needs to be placed where and on whom it belongs. Guilt is related to what you have done.

Shame is related to who you are. Shame is healed as you come to understand who you are in Christ. You are a son or daughter of the King of heaven. When this revelation seeps into your understanding, the problem of shame disappears as you see you have nothing to be ashamed of in this fundamental relationship. You are special, planned, and have a hope and a future.

For addictive thinkers, events that would normally cause guilt can be distorted into feelings of shame. Remember, guilt relates to behavior and can always be dealt with through repentance. It may be your feelings of powerlessness that help transfer these feelings into shame, but this again is a distortion of reality because in your relationship with God "all things are possible" (Matt. 19:26).

The truth

"God sent forth His Son, born of a woman, born under the law, to redeem those who were under the law, that we might receive the adoption as sons. And because you are sons, God has sent forth the Spirit of His Son into your hearts, crying out, 'Abba, Father!'" (Gal. 4:4–6). There is no shame in your relationship with God. "We have obtained an inheritance, being predestined according to the purpose of Him who works all things according to the counsel of His will" (Eph. 1:11).

Confusing responsibility

You may come up with amazingly weird ideas as to why your behavior is justified, and believe them. Sometimes your thinking may be so distorted you can even reverse the truth by saying something like, "I only drink because you're so angry with me for drinking!"

The truth

"Do not be deceived, God is not mocked; for whatever a man sows, that he will also reap" (Gal. 6:7). God will lead you into right thinking as you humble yourself and ask for His help. You may also need trusted others to help you see the truth.

Avoiding conflict

At some level addictive behavior is a method of avoiding either external or internal conflict. Research shows people with addictive behavior problems do not face more conflict than anyone else, even though they think they do. It is just that they have not learned to deal with conflict in a healthy way. Of course addictive behavior does create added conflict both internally and externally, but the person rarely admits this until they are ready to change.

The truth

Here again is avoidance of the truth (Ps. 51: 6). You are required to confront sin in yourself and others. "If your brother sins against you, rebuke him; and if he repents, forgive him" (Luke 17:3). This also points out your need to forgive yourself if you have sinned. You may need a counselor to help you learn assertion skills and healthy ways to deal with conflict.

Obsessive and compulsive thinking

This is when thoughts overtake your rational thinking and seem to take hold of you. Your desire to perform addictive behavior may become so intense that all else is swept into the background.

The truth

"Seek first the kingdom of God and His righteousness" (Matt. 6:33). "Whatever you do, do all to the glory of God" (1 Cor. 10:31). If you are plagued by obsessive thoughts, find new, creative, and healthy ways to divert your thinking. It may be helpful once again to seek advice from a counselor.

Timing

You are refusing to delay gratification. You have a "now" mentality and refuse to look at long-term consequences. You need to learn to wait for rewards and to wait to feel satisfaction. The Alcoholics Anonymous concept of "one day at a time" is essential to making progress.

The truth

"To everything there is a season, A time for every purpose under heaven" (Eccles. 3:1). Sometimes you will not know the right timing and you must accept the pain of waiting and the disappointment this can bring. "It is not for you to know times or seasons which the Father has put in His own authority" (Acts 1:7). Remember, that if you remain open and obedient, if it is God's will, it will come to pass in His timing.

Oversensitivity

Addictive behavior is a method of avoidance, and it can often be used to avoid taking responsibility for your emotions. Drugs, eating, alcohol, sex, or almost anything can be used to hide from unpleasant feelings instead of working through them. You may find yourself overreacting in situations, feeling extreme anger or hurt. You need help to label, acknowledge, and even allow yourself to feel appropriate emotions on your road to recovery. Taking responsibility in this area has a major impact on your speed of progress.

The truth

Once again God requires you to face balanced truth. Speaking about your feelings with friends can help. "Where there is no counsel, the people fall; But in the multitude of counselors there is safety" (Prov. 11:14). Keeping a journal about your feelings is a good way to explore and experiment.

Sabotage

Worrying about possible disaster, negative expectations, and thoughts that you "can't make it" may slow your progress. Others around need to bring encouragement as these forms of thinking are overcome. Share your thoughts. Humble yourself and ask for help.

The truth

'It is your Father's good pleasure to give you the kingdom' (Luke 12:32). "Whatever things are true, whatever things are noble, whatever things are just, whatever things are pure, whatever things are lovely, whatever things are of good report, if there is any virtue and if there is anything praiseworthy—meditate on these things" (Phil. 4:8). Learn to thank God and be grateful for His blessings. Practice every day.

Manipulation

With all these methods of addictive thinking occurring, it is easy to see how you can become an expert at manipulating others. It's how you keep everything under control so you do not need to face the truth and change. Unless this lying and manipulation is dealt with severely, it can become an ingrained character trait. Sadly you not only con others, you also con yourself.

The truth

"Let your 'Yes' be 'Yes,' and your 'No,' 'No.' For whatever is more than these is from the evil one" (Matt. 5:37). Dare yourself to stop lying. Share the truth with at least one friend and determine to keep telling the truth no matter what. Lying is a habit that must be broken. This doesn't mean everyone needs to know everything about you, but there are honest ways to avoid telling people what you feel they have no business knowing.

Extremes in perception

Addictive thinkers can feel helpless one moment, and the next, put all their efforts into maintaining control over people and their environment. Overall, addictive behavior is a sad attempt to maintain control over events or feelings that you do not want to accept as reality. You need to admit your powerlessness—it is real. And admit you do not have control. The reality is you have allowed the addictive behavior to take control of you.

The truth

Jesus says, "Without Me you can do nothing" (John 15:5), and "With God all things are possible" (Matt. 19:26). God is in control even though He doesn't always do things the way you would like Him to! By putting yourself under His control you are also putting yourself under His protection, guidance, love, and care. There is no better or safer place to be.

Failure to admit mistakes

Addictive thinkers have difficulty admitting when they are wrong. You are skilled at coming up with wonderfully sounding justifications for your behavior. You need to learn that it is all right not to be perfect. You are in the process of growing emotionally, mentally, and spiritually, and you will make mistakes. Sometimes the fastest way to recovery is to backtrack and admit your faults so that you can make healthy progress.

The truth

"Confess your trespasses to one another, and pray for one another, that you may be healed" (James 5:16). Everyone makes mistakes. You are not alone. It is the mature people who admit it!

Repression

Repression is a subconscious mechanism that keeps you from being aware of an unacceptable emotion. While some people have bouts of rage, others claim they are never angry. Anger, for them, is not an acceptable emotion so it is repressed. Addictive behavior can be used to help keep these emotions undercover; the behavior being used as an alternative response rather than the unwanted emotion. For example, when confronted, instead of dealing with the conflict, you may resort to drinking or abusive behavior to avoid it. If you are drunk or obnoxious you are not available for real relationship. This mechanism can backfire with repressed anger eventually bursting out in bouts of uncontrollable rage.

The truth

Again it is facing the truth in your innermost being (see Ps. 51:6). Ask the Holy Spirit to lead you into truth. "He, the Spirit of truth, has come, He will guide you into all truth; for He will not speak on His own authority, but whatever He hears He will speak" (John 16:13). As the feelings come to the surface, write about them in your journal, speak about them to a friend, and share them with God, asking how you need to respond in a healthy way. Watch other healthy people and see how they respond. It is OK to cry, to be afraid of real danger, and to be sad when something bad happens. Allow yourself to feel the pain.

Building walls

Emotional walls are built to protect you from unwanted intrusion, reinforcing isolation. You may build them by using obnoxious behavior, such as manipulation, moodiness, and lying to push people away. The behavior may even become extreme, such as using physical abuse.

The walls may be built to protect from the possibility of rejection, but this expectation of rejection can also cause you to set yourself up so that rejection becomes a self-fulfilling prophecy. You hide, but your hiding means you cannot be known and so you cannot build healthy relationships. Meeting with a small group may help here, where you can build safety, allowing you to explore some of these feelings in preparation for going out into the world to be more fully known.

Building unhealthy emotional walls is different from developing and living within healthy boundaries, as the latter are flexible and necessary for maintaining life-giving relationships.

The truth

"For He Himself is our peace, who has made both one, and has broken down the middle wall of separation, having abolished in His flesh the enmity…to create in Himself one new man from the two, thus making peace" (Eph. 2:14–15). Christ is in the business of taking down unhealthy walls. As you face the truth and decide to take responsibility for your feelings He will help you take the walls down one brick at a time.

Managing feelings

Learning how to manage newly felt feelings can be a major learning curve as you recover from addictive behavior. Feelings that were previously repressed are once again felt very strongly. If depression was one of the reasons you fell into the addiction trap, then those feelings will return until the underlying cause of them is dealt with. This can be confusing and the cause of some anxiety in the process of recovery. You may feel out of control. We will look at this in more detail in a later chapter, but for now it is important to realize that acknowledging and feeling all your emotions is an important step in your healing.

The truth

"When I was a child, I spoke as a child, I understood as a child, I thought as a child; but when I became a man, I put away childish things" (1 Cor. 13:11). God says, "I will heal their backsliding…I will be like the dew to Israel; He shall grow like a lily, And lengthen his roots like Lebanon" (Hosea 14:4–5). God will lead you at the pace you can handle. Trust Him.

Distortion of reality

Sometimes reality seems unacceptable. At least this is how it feels. This is likely to be part of the reason you began addictive behavior in the first place. Life just isn't "good enough," your expectations have not been met, or your hopes and dreams not realized. You may have refused to feel sad about very real events and instead dulled the pain by gambling, drinking, or taking drugs as a way to alleviate the bad feelings. No one likes to feel deep, painful emotions, but nevertheless they are a part of life and God has a plan for them. We will look at this in more detail in a later chapter. Overcoming this refusal to face life's ups and downs requires a determined look at reality and a determined effort to accept life as it is. Yes, life is sometimes sad, people will not always live up to your expectations, your dreams are not always fulfilled in the technicolor you desire, and sometimes life is disappointing and even boring. This is life! It is a tapestry of various possibilities woven into an intricately beautiful pattern that you cannot yet fully see.

The truth

God's plans are good. "I know the thoughts that I think toward you, says the LORD, thoughts of peace and not of evil, to give you a future and a hope" (Jer. 29:11). It can be very confusing in the middle of what seems like chaos. However, in spite of appearances, it is not chaos. God knows what He is doing, even if He does not always tell you!

Spiritual thirst

Perhaps you have been unaware of or have refused to acknowledge where your deep thirst comes from. It is a God-given thirst to draw you to Him. By refusing to acknowledge this you can set yourself up to move from one addiction to another instead of going to the Source of all life for your satisfaction.

The truth

"As the deer pants for the water brooks, So pants my soul for You, O God. My soul thirsts for God, for the living God" (Ps. 42:1–2). God made you with your thirsts so that He can fulfill them as you come to Him in deep dependence.

Changing the deceitful ways of addictive thinking is a process of change. You will need trusted friends, family, or a counselor to help you identify many of these unhelpful areas of thinking in your life. The only way to change false beliefs or deceitful thinking is to exchange them with the truth. False beliefs are lies. God is always gracious. He will help as you step out in faith. If you make mistakes, pick yourself up and keep going. A relapse does not mean you need to start again at the beginning.

A relapse into addictive behavior will always be preceded by a relapse into addictive thinking. Check your thinking if you suspect it is moving off track! Replace the lie with the truth.

GETTING REAL

Pray and ask God to show you areas where your thinking is unhealthy. Listen to the conviction of the Holy Spirit and be honest with yourself. If you are still unsure, ask those close to you. They will tell you!

In what areas do I need to change my thinking?

How can I change these areas? (What truths do I need to exchange them with?)

Do I need to go to a Christian counselor for help?

If so, ask around and make an appointment today.

Write a statement or paragraph about why you want to stop your addictive behavior.

Chapter Six

THROUGH THE VALLEY OF THE SHADOW OF DEATH

How gaily a man wakes in the morning to watch himself keep on dying.[1]
—HENRY S. HASKINS

Facing reality can be hard. Life can be very painful. One of the major problems you may face in your journey away from bondage to addictive behavior is your intense fear of pain. This fear may have been the motivation that propelled you towards addictive behavior in the first place, but nevertheless the fear needs to be faced for recovery to succeed.

King David wrote about this painful journey of facing fear and coming to terms with life's reality in Psalm 23. Let's look closely at what he discovered:

Yea, though I walk through the valley of the shadow of death; I will fear no evil; For You are with me; Your rod and Your staff, they comfort me. —PSALM 23:4

When pain seems overwhelming, you are walking through this "valley of the shadow of death." You may fear it is death and that if you walk here you will lose your life. However looking closely at David's writing we find he calls it the valley of the *shadow of death.* It is not real death. It is only death's shadow.

In Scripture real death is described as separation from God. It involves a death of soul and spirit in relationship with God. Through personal choices you can turn your back on God refusing His gift of salvation and be vanquished to a place where God does not abide. It is a place devoid of all the wonderful characteristics of God—His love, joy, peace, light, goodness, holiness, justice, righteousness, relationship, and comfort. Jesus describes it as a place of "outer darkness. There will be weeping and gnashing of teeth" (Matt. 8:12).

In contrast, this valley you are called to walk in is not the valley of death just described, even though Satan will whisper in your ear that it is. Remember Satan is a liar (see John 8:44). He lied to Adam and Eve and he is lying to you if this is what you think. Instead of real death you are asked to walk in the valley of the shadow of death. We know this is not real death (separation from God), because David tells us "For You are with me." This means that God is here. He is not absent. Because of this there is nothing to fear. You are in a place for a purpose and God is with you to help and guide you.

To add more light, perhaps you are familiar with the concept of the "shadow self." It refers to the part of you that is not good, the part that is capable of evil. The Bible calls this part the "old man" or the "flesh." And Roman 8:13 says, "if you live according to the flesh you will die." Now let's see how these two concepts fit together.

You are asked to walk through the valley of the shadow of death—remember this is not real death—and in the process as you walk here, God deals with your "shadow self," that part of you that is not good, that is capable of evil.

How does He do this? What is He doing in this valley with you? David explains, "Your rod and Your staff, they comfort me." God's rod and staff refer to His discipline and guidance. In this valley of the shadow of death God is disciplining and guiding you. Why is He doing this? He wants to make you more like His Son Jesus Christ. "For whom the LORD loves He chastens, And scourges every son whom He receives" (Heb. 12:6). "Now no chastening seems to be joyful for the present, but painful; nevertheless, afterward it yields the peaceable fruit of righteousness to those who have been trained by it" (Heb. 12:11).

Walking though the valley of the shadow of death with God at your side disciplining and comforting you will result in the death of your shadow side—the death of your flesh. Jesus Christ died on the cross to make this possible.

With this death of your sinful disposition and your flesh you will find your wrong attachments also die. These wrong attachments are what set you up for addictive behavior.

Yes, it can be a very painful process, but you are not alone, God promises to be with you, to comfort you and show you the way. His staff will guide you. Because it is only the valley of the shadow of death and not real death, you will find that as you walk through it, it is in fact the pathway to life!

What you lose in the process are those things that are not part of God's will for your life; things that are worthless and hinder you from experiencing all God has to offer. He wants you free to walk in victory in His kingdom. The things you lose hold you back from this even though you may find them comforting because they are familiar. Remember Jesus said He came to give us life and to give it more abundantly (see John 10:10). You don't need extra baggage weighing you down, stopping you from enjoying this new life. It is time to let it go.

The valley of the shadow of death is a place of death. It's the place where the sin and unhelpful distractions in your life need to die. This is your sanctification. It is something you already have in Christ (see 1 Cor. 1:30), and the more you enter into it the more fulfilled you will feel. Oswald Chambers said:

> *The one marvelous secret of the holy life lies not in imitat-*
> *ing Jesus, but in letting the perfections of Jesus manifest*

> *themselves in my mortal flesh. It is "Christ in You." It is His*
> *wonderful life that is imparted by faith as a sovereign gift*
> *of God's grace. Sanctification is not drawing from Jesus the*
> *power to be holy; it is drawing from Jesus the holiness that*
> *was manifested in Him, and He manifests it in me…all*
> *the perfections of Jesus are at my disposal, and slowly and*
> *surely I begin to live a life of ineffable order and sanity and*
> *holiness: "Kept in the power of God."[2]*

As you accept what Jesus has already done, you will leave the old life like a butterfly leaving its chrysalis and you will learn to fly. The struggle of the butterfly to leave the chrysalis is your walk through the valley of the shadow of death. And the release as it spreads its wings is your victory into life.

Walking through the valley of the shadow of death means facing up to truth. This includes the reality of your past, the reality of your mistakes, the knowledge of where you really are now, and how you fall short of God's glory. It means facing up to the losses you have experienced in life and seeing them clearly for what they are. And it means grieving these losses as a way towards inner healing. We will look further into the grieving process in a later chapter.

There can also be another reason why you need to walk through this difficult valley of the shadow of death. As weird as it may sound, Peter tells us: "Do not think it strange concerning the fiery trial which is to try you, as though some strange thing happened to you; but rejoice to the extent that you partake of Christ's sufferings, that when His glory is revealed, you also may be glad with exceeding joy" (1 Pet. 4:12).

We all suffer at some point in our lives. It is never a question of "if," but of "how," and possibly "when." If you are held in bondage by addictive behavior, you are refusing to acknowledge this and live through it. Instead you are rebelling and deciding to find your own way to fulfillment by trying to avoid the suffering that is a part of everyone's life. But of course, as you have already discovered, this doesn't work, because in the end addictive behavior results in its own form of suffering.

There is a marvelous result of walking through the valley of the shadow of death. David declares God has prepared a wonderful victory celebration:

> *You prepare a table before me in the presence of my enemies; You anoint my head with oil; My cup runs over. Surely goodness and mercy shall follow me All the days of my life; And I will dwell in the house of the LORD Forever.*
> —PSALM 23:5–6

The anointing of your head with oil is the leading, guiding, empowering, and healing of the Holy Spirit as you reach out to God. And your cup overflowing is the result of your walk through the valley as the benefits of your healing and growth overflow into other people's lives. Your enemies will be amazed at the changed and fulfilled life they see in you and you will be able to step out in faith, walking in righteousness as you are blessed by God forever.

GETTING REAL

Am I allowing myself to walk through the valley of the shadow of death, or am I avoiding it by being busy or using some other distraction?

What are some of the parts in me that need to die?

Do these parts honor God? Am I willing to let them go?

If not, why not?

If you are still struggling, ask God to help you become willing to allow these parts to die.

Chapter Seven

DISCOVERING YOUR FEELINGS

Emotion has taught mankind to reason.[1]
—MARQUIS DE VAUVENARGUES

Getting in touch with repressed feelings is an important part of recovery. God gave us feelings so we can relate to others. The feelings in themselves are neither good nor bad, they are just there. And they are important indicators that can be used as data to help explore what is really going on within and to assist in making wise decisions. However, it is important not to be ruled by your emotions as often they are linked with past events and may not be relevant for today. This is why I call them indicators to use as data. They do not necessarily reflect reality.

Sometimes due to difficult circumstances in early childhood, certain feelings are deemed unacceptable. For example, if you were continually scolded or punished for showing displeasure, you may have subconsciously decided anger is unacceptable. Now in adult life you may never feel angry. It doesn't matter what people do or how badly they treat you, you take it with a smile, perhaps even secretly thinking you deserve it. However, no matter how skillfully you try to hide and repress your anger, there is always a place inside that knows the truth, and this place keeps making itself known. If you determine to stay in denial, you are likely to fall into depression, which will remain until the real issues are properly dealt with. There is nothing wrong with being angry when you are treated unjustly. Anger is an appropriate response. The question is, How can you express your anger and remain safe?

Or perhaps you are afraid to trust and be vulnerable with your spouse because in your childhood any form of tenderness and love was met with scorn and ridicule, and you fear that if you reveal this part of you, it will be abused. If you were brought up in an abusive family, protecting this part of you by hiding it was sensible. You needed to hide it to survive. But now that you are an adult this defensive mechanism is no longer useful. In fact it may be destroying the most important relationships in your life. But how, you may ask, can you lower your defenses and remain safe?

Or maybe you have been so successful at repressing your feelings that you don't feel anything! You live in a dull, bland world of mediocrity; a place you have decided is safe! Yet this is not life—it is a form of slow, draining death.

If your addiction started in adolescence you may also discover your emotions were frozen at that time and the process of healing may involve going back to those outbursts of emotions typical of teenage years and then maturing through the stages of normal development. God is gracious at such times and instead of the long steady growth of a tree that maturity is often likened to, He can cause you to grow quickly like a lily. (see Hos. 14:5). It will be at a pace you can accommodate.

Now is the time to dare to begin to live and feel the depths of your emotions again and to learn how to manage feelings of anger, insecurity, and fear. Let's look at some steps you can take:

Step one

Get a large piece of paper and write down as many feelings as you can think of. Keep going until you have at least twenty.

Step two

Decide where in your body you feel each emotion. For example, fear is often felt in the pit of the stomach while love is felt in the chest. If you don't know, ask a friend where they feel these feelings in their body.

Step three

Think of an instance when you have felt each emotion. If you can't recall one, then think of a situation where it would be appropriate to have these feelings. Imagine yourself in the situation and let the emotions flow. Remember you are sitting safely in your chair. If the emotions become too intense, stand up and recite your name and address. This will bring you back into the present.

Step four

Check in with yourself every hour throughout the day and identify how you are feeling. Label the emotion and note what it feels like in your body. Give yourself permission to feel. For example, disappointment may feel like a sinking in your stomach. Allow the feeling; see what happens to it.

Step five

Start a journal and write about your feelings every day. As you become more familiar with them you will be able to write less frequently, but it's important to take time to do this as it will help you explore the depths of your emotions without taking them out on others.

Step six

Make a decision to take responsibility for your feelings. This is essential so you do not cause yourself or others harm. You may wonder how this is done. Anger, for example, is an appropriate response to injustice, but this does not mean it is appropriate to physically abuse the person you are angry with.

Instead, it may be appropriate to confront them directly in a firm, but calm, manner through learning assertion skills, or in serious cases, to contact authorities, such as the police or a lawyer. Or if you are disappointed, it may be wise to voice your feelings openly and honestly without sulking, withdrawing, or trying to punish the person for not doing what you want. They are responsible for their behavior, actions, and feelings and you are for yours. It is not kind or wise to try and control others with your moods. This is manipulation. The process of taking responsibility for emotions takes time. You may need honest feedback from others to determine the best response in differing situations as you grow in maturity

Learning to own, understand, and take responsibility for emotions is an adventurous task. You will experience ups and downs and may even feel overwhelmed, but be gentle with yourself. Give yourself time. You won't get it right every instance. If you make a mistake, recognize it as soon as possible, own it, apologize, and carry on. Keep telling yourself the truth. Emotions are generally the result of thoughts. If your thinking is wrong (addictive thinking) your emotions are likely to be inappropriate. As you replace lies with the truth, your emotions will come closer into balance with reality. Emotions are data to help you make wise decisions. They are not intended to dominate your life, so don't let them.

You may also have to interact with people who are not taking responsibility for their feelings. Don't let this put you off. If they refuse to respect your boundaries then gently protect and even remove yourself until they do. You will get the level of respect from others that you allow, and put into action by letting your boundaries be known.

GETTING REAL

Am I in touch with my feelings?

Which feelings do I think are wrong? Have I repressed these feelings?

Can I identify emotional responses in my body?

Will I give myself permission to experience these feelings?

Who is suffering because of my feelings? (Either repressed or overly expressed)

What can I do to take responsibility for these feelings so that others do not suffer?

Chapter Eight

GRIEVING YOUR LOSSES

*I dip my pen in the blackest ink, because I
am not afraid of falling into my inkpot.*[1]
—RALPH WALDO EMERSON

Walking through the valley of the shadow of death, uncovering repressed feelings, and accepting the truth about your past will result in the discovery of losses you have experienced throughout your life. These losses can be as varied as individual experiences. Perhaps you never received unconditional love from a parent. Perhaps you have spent most of your life repressing your emotions because of childhood trauma and now feel you were cheated of emotional depth. Perhaps your innocence was stolen or you were never allowed to be you. All of these are losses, resulting in the stripping away of something that was rightly yours. Your needs were not met by significant people, and you have suffered as a consequence.

These losses are real and for you to be healed and become whole, they cannot be ignored. Instead, they must be acknowledged and, if necessary, grieved. If you try to skirt around the edges and pretend they don't matter, they may resurface in the future, causing further pain. You may also need to face truth if you are implicated in the loss. In Jeremiah 5:3, God displays His desire for truth in this area. "O LORD, are not Your eyes on the truth? You have stricken them, But they have not grieved; You have consumed them, But they have refused to receive correction." Yet even in this, God's compassion shines through (see Lam. 3:23).

However, even if you are not implicated and the loss was out of your control, you are not alone. Jesus was described as "despised and rejected by men, A Man of sorrows and acquainted with grief" (Isa. 53:3). Even when God brings correction into your life it causes Him grief. He said, "Woe is me for my hurt! My wound is severe. But I say, 'Truly this is an infirmity, And I must bear it'" (Jer. 10:19). Grief is a part of everyone's life. King Solomon declared that "each one knows his own burden and his own grief" (2 Chron. 6:29).

The best way to achieve deep healing is to walk through the grief, going through the pain it brings to the surface. And wonderfully God has not left you alone to do this. He has given the grief process, which, when worked through, will bring you to a place of real healing and wholeness. The process affects each person differently; however, psychologists have identified many typical stages.

Initially shock and denial may hit as you scarcely believe what is happening. They allow you to absorb harsh reality in a buffered way so that you can cope. You may feel numb, stunned, or disorientated. It is a way to delay the unpleasant impact of reality. Slowly the truth will begin to dawn and you need to acknowledge this gradually, facing the reality of your circumstances. We have looked at the acceptance of truth already in this book.

With reality seeping into your consciousness, you may experience physical feelings of emotional pain that accompany these truths and they will swirl through your body. King David cried out "my eye wastes away because of grief" (Ps. 6:7). Allow the emotional release they bring in waves of pain, tears, or sobs. Learn to express your emotions safely.

You may also experience various bodily reactions accompanying these feelings such as physical pain, sleep disturbances, and variances in bodily function. You may eat more or less or need to use the bathroom more or less as you adjust. All these reactions are a normal part of the grief process as the truth sinks deeply into your soul. Look after yourself gently as you pass through this stage. You may need extra rest or sleep. Treat yourself with hot bubble baths, long walks on the beach, or movies with chocolate dipped ice cream. Give yourself permission to nurture yourself.

As reality hits, you may find yourself slowly walking through a deep valley of depression and even panic. Job said, "Oh, that my grief were fully weighed, And my calamity laid with it on the scales! For then it would be heavier than the sand of the sea" (Job 6:2–3). The tunnel may appear endless, like a long nightmare, but there is light on the other side. Keep walking and you will reach it. Look after yourself carefully, remembering that many others have walked this path before and can testify that it doesn't last so long as you keep moving. You do this by allowing yourself to feel the depths of emotion, and determining to face new truth as it presents itself. You may need to put time aside to cry, time to be alone and mull over the terrible, sad truths you are discovering about yourself and others. Don't get stuck; keep walking. Depression will not linger if you stay with the process, it is only when you refuse to face truth and move on that you can get stuck. Serious depression can bring feelings of hopelessness and helplessness, but if you are on a journey these feelings will not last. Remember you have a purpose even if you cannot see the end result right now.

You may also face feelings of guilt, and need to decide whether they are imagined or real. If guilt is real, you are implicated and must take responsibility for your part in the problem. You will need to repent and make restitution where possible. If it is unrealistic guilt, such as when you take on the guilt of another or blame yourself for something you had no control over, then you need to release it, or assign it to the appropriate person if it is displaced.

Anger may threaten to overwhelm you at times through the process—anger at others, at God, and at yourself. You will resent having something precious taken away from you and need to acknowledge and safely express this anger without causing further harm. Pray it out, shout it out to God, or write about it and when you feel calmer share it with a friend.

However, even after all these stages are worked through in their billowing cycles, the process is not complete because your mind may still play tricks and you could find yourself idealizing your situation. Through your glazed thinking you may see the relationship or job as "the best" and feel nothing could match it again. Or perhaps you see it as "the worst." It takes time for reality to set in. If the past had its good and bad, then the future can also be seen to have the potential for both good and bad.

Once this stage of truth and reality thinking is reached, you are ready to start looking at new patterns of living. These may entail learning new skills, taking risks, trying new behaviors, and over time you will come to the place where you can successfully live with your loss.

Isaiah 53:4 says, "[Jesus] has borne [your] griefs And carried [your] sorrows." He did this when He died on the cross in your place and yet, as with physical illness, there are seasons when you will walk this path. The grieving process is rarely clear-cut and bounces around as new truths and perceptions are added. Go with the flow; don't be discouraged if it seems to be taking a long time. And don't listen to insensitive people who tell you to "get over it and get on with life." The average time to work through serious loss can be two years. Give yourself space.

Even in the end, the memories are still there, the loss is real, but you will be able to look back without an unwelcome outpouring of emotion. You may bear the scars, but the wound will be healed.

GETTING REAL

What losses do I need to acknowledge from my past?

What suffering has my addictive behavior caused in my life?

What suffering has it caused in the lives of others?

Am I working through the grief process?

Am I stuck at one stage of the process? (If so, you may need to seek a counselor for help.)

Chapter Nine

TIMING

Life is what happens to us while
we are making other plans.[1]
—THOMAS LA MANCE

Rarely do things happen exactly when we want them to. And we are left disappointed, sometimes disillusioned, and almost always frustrated. We may try harder to make them happen or we may give up. Whichever we chose, we end up waiting. The world rejects waiting. It causes pain. "Give me patience and give it quick!" can be the heart's cry. We long for instant gratification. And in some things we get it!

We have instant coffee, frozen dinners, microwaves, and digital cameras, to name a few, but there are other things that don't come this way no matter how much we wish they would. There's no such thing as an instant relationship or instant intimacy. Relationships take time to grow and build. Love takes time to mature. Real intimacy takes time to enjoy. Writing about those suffering under sexual addiction in his book False Intimacy, Dr. Harry W. Schaumburg said, "Addicts' actions are self centered...the persistent drive to become involved in that behavior demonstrates a lack of concern for others... Ultimately meeting their own needs is most important...the key to understanding addictive behavior is that sex addict's

59

demand to have safety, control relational pain, and satisfaction causes them to behave in ways that defy their own reason and values—often with disastrous results."[2]

This statement is true of all addictive behavior. The unhealthy behavior is an attempt to have perceived needs met under your control—now, without waiting. It is a refusal to bow under God's sovereignty and will, to wait for God's perfect timing, and to grow spiritually, especially in at least one of the fruits of the Spirit—patience.

God's timing is a mystery. Even the words He uses, as they are translated into English, clearly show that God's concept of timing is different from ours. There are times when God uses words that mean one thing to us but quite another thing to Him. In his book, *Prophets and Personal Prophecy*, Dr. Bill Hamon points to examples:[3]

> *"Immediately" means from one day to three years.*
>
> *"Very soon" means one to ten years.*
>
> *"Now" or "This day" means one to forty years.*
>
> *"I will" without a time designation means God will act sometime in the person's life if he is obedient.*
>
> *"Soon" was the term Jesus used to describe the time of His 'soon' return almost two thousand years ago.*

It is easy to see that God is very patient and He wants you to be patient also. In Romans 15:5 He is called the "God of patience." He is never in a hurry and although He often seems to wait until the last minute, He is never late in achieving what He wants to achieve. And here is where the problem lies. Sometimes what you think you need is not what God knows is best for you. It helps to remember that God always wants the best for you, not just what seems good in your eyes. He loves you too much to allow you to successfully carry on your own destructive path. And in His mysterious way, God has so arranged the universe so that what is best for you will also be what glorifies His name.

Learning to wait can be one of the hardest lessons you need to learn. However, let's face it, you actually spend your whole life waiting. As soon as you receive one thing it's not long before you have something else in mind that you want, and the waiting game starts all over again, from one thing to the next, year in, year out. At the end of our lives some will even sit waiting to die!

For your own peace of mind and to be able to enjoy life fully, you need to learn how to wait well and joyfully. And this, of course, takes practice! James says to "count it all joy when you fall into various trials, knowing that the testing of your faith produces patience. But let patience have its perfect work, that you may be perfect and complete, lacking nothing" (James 1:3–4).

Earlier this year, when suffering from the flu and a chest infection, I prayed for healing. It didn't happen. I knew God could heal because He has miraculously healed me more than once in the past. I knew scriptures that promised His healing and I prayed them faithfully many times a day. I also asked others to pray for me, but still my healing didn't come. I knew I had the revelation, I had the faith, and I believed. I asked continually, but still nothing happened. I finally asked God why, and He made it very clear there was one thing I had forgotten. All my works, my doings, my prayers, my words, even my faith would not produce the results without God's timing also being perfectly in line. Everything we receive is by grace. Jesus said, "Without Me you can do nothing" (John 15:5). He is right. God will not give up His sovereignty to anyone! All my praying, believing, and hoping will not make anything happen if it does not line up with God's perfect timing and will. However, I am not suggesting you sit back and do nothing. There is also a part you need to play.

When praying for deliverance from addictive behavior by walking in the Spirit with God's help, you need to obey all you know, and leave the timing up to God. Of course, if you are sincere, He is willing and your sincerity will give you the strength to do the waiting required. The waiting will strengthen your faith and produce a new depth of character. As Schaumberg points out: "[You] can choose to trust God to help [you] respond honorably to the pain in [your] heart and [your] desires for personal satisfaction, regardless of the confusion and disappointment life brings."[4] It is a matter of walking through the pain and trusting God to help you. This part of trusting is your choice, yet even in this you will need God's grace.

GETTING REAL

Am I prepared to wait for things in my life?

In what areas do I refuse to wait?

Why do I refuse? What is happening in my heart?

Am I prepared to suffer the pain of learning to wait for God's perfect timing?

Chapter Ten

GOD'S GRACE

*Grace … is an outpouring, a boundless
burning offering of God's self to us suffering
with us, overflowing with tenderness.
Grace is God's passion.*[1]
—GERALD MAY

God's timing is a function of His grace, just like everything else you receive from Him. You cannot even obey without His grace operating in your life. You cannot recover from the destructive effects of addiction without the help of His grace. As Gerald May points out in *Addiction and Grace*, "Grace is our only hope for dealing with addiction, the only power that can truly vanquish its destructiveness. Grace is the invincible advocate of freedom and the absolute expression of perfect love."[2]

You desperately need God's help to enter into the fullness of relationship He offers you, and you need it to enter into the fullness of relationship He offers you with others. Addiction stops your love for God and others from being complete. It short-circuits the process, holding you in bondage to other gods—gods you have placed in supremacy in your life by your choices. It is only through partaking of the gift of grace, entering deeply into repentance, and making new choices that change will occur in your life.

Even though your will is seriously damaged and eroded through continual addictive behavior, there is always some level at which a choice is still available to you. It is at this point that you must avail yourself of God's grace. And "hope does not disappoint, because the love of God has been poured out in our hearts" (Rom. 5:5).

God's grace is also needed to assist where your self-esteem has been seriously damaged. Continual failure to make healthy choices erodes self-esteem, and this can only be reestablished through God's gracious affirmation of you as His beloved child, regardless of your behavior. This accepting grace is not a license to continue in sin—it is an encouragement to follow God's leading and obey His word.

You will grow spiritually as you become aware of your need for God's grace and mercy. This spiritual growth will enable you to make right choices. Gerald May also makes the observation that true love is always born of a difficult choice. This is true in your love for God as well as your love for fellow humans. Take a marriage relationship for example. For a marriage to be healthy and continue to grow in satisfaction and fulfillment, each partner must make a choice every day to remain faithful, vulnerable, and open to their partner. This choice must be made even in times of severe difficulty—through sleepless nights, illness, financial strain, and temptations. There is always another alternative to follow, an alternative that does not glorify God. There is always a way out, but for a marriage to be strong, the choice to stay and love must be made continually.

This choice is also true in your relationship with God. If you want a fulfilling, strong, maturing spiritual life and relationship with God you must make the choice to commune with and obey Him every day. The same is true in overcoming sin in your life. The choice has to be made every day and, in some cases, every moment. There are no shortcuts to reaching the freedom you desire and are offered. It involves a choice of yielding to God's will, a yielding to His ways, and a yielding to

His love. Every moment you need to rely on God's grace and every moment you need to obey. Your obedience is the fruit of your yielding, regardless of the cost to yourself. It is done in the belief that God has your best interests at heart, that He knows what He is doing, and that there is nothing He will ask you to do that He will not also provide all you need to succeed. Your choices need to be made trusting Him to provide the grace when you need it.

Grace is not a one-way street. Yes, it originates in God and you can do nothing without Him. But there is a response you must make. In 1 Peter the disciple signs off stating, "this is the true grace of God in which you stand" (1 Peter 5:12). If you carefully read the Book of 1 Peter, you will find clear statements of God's faithfulness, purpose, and grace.

> *Our Lord Jesus Christ, who according to His abundant mercy has begotten us again to a living hope through the resurrection of Jesus Christ from the dead, to an inheritance incorruptible and undefiled and that does not fade away, reserved in heaven for you, who are kept by the power of God through faith for salvation.* —1 PETER 1:3–5

You will also find clear instructions on the part you need to play to live in this grace:

> **Conduct yourselves** *throughout the time of your stay here in fear.* —1 PETER 1:17, EMPHASIS ADDED

> *Since* **you have purified** *your souls* **in obeying** *the truth through the Spirit…love one another fervently with a pure heart.* —1 PETER 1:22, EMPHASIS ADDED

> **Laying aside** *all malice, all deceit, hypocrisy, envy, and all evil speaking.* —1 PETER 2:1, EMPHASIS ADDED

> *Abstain from fleshly lusts.*
> —1 PETER 2:11, EMPHASIS ADDED

> *Submit yourselves to every ordinance of man for the Lord's sake.* —1 PETER 2:13, EMPHASIS ADDED

> *Not using liberty as a cloak for vice.*
> —1 PETER 2:16, EMPHASIS ADDED

> *Turn away from evil and do good…seek peace and pursue it.* —1 PETER 3:11, EMPHASIS ADDED

There are many more examples, all included in Peter's definition of the true grace of God.

It becomes clear that your walk of grace, and walking in the Spirit, entail a layering effect or passage of growth. As God gives grace, you receive it in obedience, and as you receive it and action it, you receive more grace for the next step. As you obey that step, you receive more, and on and on it goes as you remain open to receiving God's grace and responding in obedience.

Gerald May once again summarizes this well. "Addiction cannot be defeated by the human will acting on its own, nor by the human will opting out and turning everything over to divine will. Instead, the power of grace flows most fully when human will chooses to act in harmony with divine will."[3]

Grace always exists—it is always available, it is always good, and it is always victorious.

You need to stay in your situation, facing the truth, determined to take responsibility for your choices, while at the same time turning to God for His grace. It is always there.

As Albert Schweitzer so aptly said, "Truth has no special time of its own. Its hour is now—always."[4]

GETTING REAL

Do you believe God's grace is available to you?

Are you availing yourself of it?

Are you responding in obedience?

If not, why not? Stop making excuses!

Chapter Eleven

TEMPTATION

There is no right way to do a wrong thing.
—AUTHOR UNKNOWN

Living by grace and by the Spirit is not always easy. You will
have times of temptation. Temptation is part of everyone's life
and is the start of any addiction. It is how you react that deter-
mines the outcome. You may believe your temptations are
worse than everyone else's, but research has shown this is not
true. Other people have just learned how to deal with temptation in a more healthy way. Scripture also upholds this:

> *No temptation has overtaken you except such as is com-
> mon to man; but God is faithful, who will not allow
> you to be tempted beyond what you are able, but with
> the temptation will also make the way of escape, that
> you may be able to bear it. —1 CORINTHIANS 10:13*

This clearly says your temptation is the same that tempts
millions of others. You need to ask the question: Why do I suc-
cumb to addiction and they don't? It's an important question,
one you may already have found an answer to in this book.
Discovering the answer means facing stark truths about yourself. If you feel none the wiser, reread this book and be more
honest with yourself. You are probably still in denial!

The above scripture also says that God is faithful and He assures you will not be tempted at a level you are unable to deal with. In other words for every temptation you receive, He guarantees to give you enough grace to resist it. The question is: Are you availing yourself of His grace to do this?

This scripture also tells you how to resist temptation. God promises to give you a "way of escape." Have you looked for it? Have you found it? Are you using it? If you don't know what it is, then ask the Holy Spirit who is living inside you to show you. If you are still unsure, ask a friend or Christian counselor to help you find it. You are guaranteed by God that it is there. And you are guaranteed you have the grace to use it. Are you willing to be obedient and do it? It may mean taking a different route home from work so you do not pass a pornography store, or not meeting certain friends in a bar but instead meeting at a café. It may mean not buying certain foods at the supermarket or not calling that person on your cell phone. The way will be there. Look for it and take it!

Sometimes the Spirit may tell you to run away. The Bible says to "flee from idolatry" (1 Cor. 10:14), and to "flee sexual immorality" (1 Cor. 6:18). God knows how weak you are in these areas. If you are continually tempted to commit adultery at work, then change jobs. It doesn't matter if you have to take a salary decrease. God will help you adjust or will provide the money you need from a different source. Obedience is the key. You are also told to flee greed (see 1 Tim. 6:10–11). This does not mean giving up work, but it may mean giving up gambling or changing your attitude toward money.

When you flee something, you don't run madly off in any direction. This will only get you into trouble of a different sort. Paul says "flee these things and pursue righteousness, godliness, faith, love, patience, gentleness" (1 Tim. 6:11). There is enough here to pursue for a lifetime!

We are also instructed to abstain from fleshly lusts (see 1 Pet. 2:11). Some fleshly lusts are very difficult to abstain from, such as food. Eating is a necessary function to survive and yet we must abstain from gluttony, overeating, and using food as a way to gain comfort or maintain control, as in anorexia. The process of maintaining a healthy balance is very difficult, but we can be wise and avoid unhelpful locations, such as favorite fast-food stores or ice-cream parlors.

It is important to note that by taking the way of escape, the temptation may not necessarily disappear, but by availing yourself of God's grace, it will lose its power over you. This is because you are choosing to walk in the Spirit instead of in the flesh. Paul said, "Walk in the Spirit, and you shall not fulfill the lust of the flesh" (Gal. 5:16).

Temptation is a test of who you are as a complete person. It is a test of your character. Thomas Babington Macauley (1800–1859) said, "The measure of a man's character is what he would do if he knew he never would be found out."[1] The test is not for God's knowledge or understanding. He already knows how you will react; the test is for you to see where you are standing. It is an opportunity for your faith, trust, and character to grow, and God uses it for this purpose.

You need to grow. Whatever is not growing is dying. There are no static positions. You are either moving towards death or life. Of course, it is possible to grow unevenly because of circumstances in your life. Leanne Payne points out, "We are more vulnerable to temptations and odd compulsions when we develop one part of our mind or personality at the expense of another."[2] However, God wants you to grow up and become whole in every area.

This truth points to the need for balance in every area of life. And it shows that temptation can be clearly viewed as an opportunity to grow. This perspective brings temptation into a positive light and encourages a responsible and obedient response.

Temptation is a place of choice. It is a crossroads where your character meets reality. You may have all the pious thoughts and beliefs in the world, but they only become real when they are put to the test. Peter said, "though now for a little while, if need be, you have been grieved by various trials, that the genuineness of your faith, being much more precious than gold that perishes, though it is tested by fire, may be found to praise, honor, and glory at the revelation of Jesus Christ" (1 Pet. 1:6–7). Ultimately you are tested to purify your faith so you will glorify and honor Christ in everything. This is another reason to look at temptation in a positive light. It helps to purify your life so you may honor Jesus.

Although the cause of many temptations is the evil desires within you (from the sinful disposition inherited from Adam), there is also a constant battle going on in the spiritual realm: "For we do not wrestle against flesh and blood, but against principalities, against powers, against the rulers of the darkness of this age, against spiritual hosts of wickedness in the heavenly places" (Eph. 6:12).

God has not left you helpless. To counteract these evil forces, God has given you two major weapons. The first is prayer. Ask others to join you, sharing in the responsibility to help make your path of growth straight by overcoming the plans of the enemy. The second is a suit of armor. Paul said, "Stand therefore, having girded your waist with truth, having put on the breastplate of righteousness, and having shod your feet with the preparation of the gospel of peace; above all, taking the shield of faith with which you will be able to quench all the fiery darts of the wicked one. And take the helmet of salvation, and the sword of the Spirit, which is the Word of God; praying always with all prayer and supplication in the Spirit" (Eph. 6:14–18).

Wearing this cumbersome armor, you may wonder how hard you are expected to fight. Amazingly, you aren't! All you need to do is stand. "Therefore take up the whole armor of God, that you may be able to withstand in the evil day, and having done all, to stand" (v. 13). That's it! You only need to stand. The battle belongs to God!

I have heard of people praying their armor on every day and

I have done it myself through difficult trials, but one day I realized I had never taken it off! The armor of God is something I now live in all the time. Yes, I prayed for it in the beginning, but now I live, eat, walk, and sleep in it. Never take it off!

Satan never changes his tricks. He will always try to tempt you, and usually at the worst moment. Even Jesus suffered under his evil schemes when He was led by the Spirit into the wilderness and tempted for forty days and forty nights. He overcame standing in God's truth. You are also instructed to "resist the devil and he will flee from you" (James 4:7). This verse has the crucial instruction for success. It begins, "submit to God," and just like Jesus, you must do this first, before you can successfully resist Satan.

As soon as you begin praying and asking God for freedom—the freedom that Christ has already won for you on the cross, the spiritual battle is underway. Don't worry if you see little progress in the beginning. The battle is won in the strategy room and the best strategy is prayer. Remember to ask others to pray for you. You need fellow soldiers to help you win this battle.

What happens if you relapse in the face of severe temptation?

It's important to understand a relapse does not mean you need to start back at the beginning. If you are a child of God, your relapse is covered by the work Jesus did on the cross. "There is therefore now no condemnation to those who are in Christ Jesus, who do not walk according to the flesh, but according to the Spirit. For the law of the Spirit of life in Christ Jesus has made me free from the law of sin and death" (Rom. 8:1–2). Remember, this does not give you a license to sin because then you are no longer walking in the Spirit. Pick yourself up, repent, and carry on, thanking God for His grace in covering you.

If you feel out of control, that the compulsion is out of your willpower to change, feeling you cannot resist, or perhaps even failing to see any reason to resist, this is because you are looking for help in the wrong place. You are made up of a body, soul, and spirit. Your soul is comprised of your mind, will, and emotions. This is the area the Bible calls the "flesh." It is where you think, feel, and desire. Remember, Paul said to walk in the Spirit and not the flesh. Your power to resist cannot be found in your soul—in your thoughts, your willpower, or your feelings. You need to be strengthened in the inner man and look to your spirit. It is here that God will give you the power you need, through the work of His Holy Spirit who lives within you. Bring your spirit into submission to God's will and His power will rise within you.

GETTING REAL

What do I do when I am tempted? Do I look for and take the "way of escape"?

How can temptation help me grow? What is my attitude towards temptation?

Do I understand what the armor of God is for?

Am I wearing it? How must I fight?

If I experience a relapse, what must I do?

Am I walking in the Spirit or in the flesh?

If I am walking in the flesh, how can I change?

Chapter Twelve

SITTING IN THE SPACE

*A contemplative quality can be found in
anyone who has encountered emptiness
and chosen not to run away.[1]*
—GERALD MAY

When resisting temptation by taking the way of escape, you
may find yourself in a strange place I call "sitting in the space."
You have resisted, and feel you deserve accolades of praise, or
at least encouragement, or in the very least, relief, but all you
find is space! It's a wide-open space that feels very unfamiliar.
It is silent and can be eerie and rather frightening. There is
an unknowingness about it, a strangeness that makes you feel
uncertain of what to expect and of what happens next. If you
have experienced this space before, you may identify it as a
similar space experienced before partaking in another bout of
addictive behavior. You need to start looking at this space in
a different light. This space comes after resistance, and it is a
place to grow.

Addictive behavior is one way to avoid this space, but people
use many other things to take away this strange space, such as
radio, television, cell phones, endless chatter, friends, sports,

busyness, or just any activity. Addictive behavior is just a more destructive method of avoiding the feelings it brings, the feelings of emptiness, and lack of control. Of course, ironically, addiction soon takes over as being out of control and the space then becomes a signal to begin another cycle. You become the slave, but there is "sick comfort" in this. In maintaining the addictive cycle there is at least a certainty. You know what to expect, whereas in this place of space, sitting in the space, you don't!

Sitting in the space is a place of contemplation; it is a place to sit in the presence of God and wait on Him. It is a place of prayer and communication with your Father in heaven. You need to learn to stay here in the position you are in and turn your heart and mind toward God to receive His grace. Then sit in the space, remaining there to receive from Him. It is a secret place of daring to trust.

Trust is a huge transition to ask of anyone under the bondage of addictive behavior. It is your lack of trust and refusal to be vulnerable that has led to addiction in the first place, but it is growth in this area that will lead you out.

Trust is built in relationship. It grows as you experience that someone is trustworthy. If you discover a person is not trustworthy, it is wise not to trust them. But your God in heaven is the most trustworthy Being in the universe, even though His ways are often mysterious. He is the rock, the foundation of all life and relationship, and He loves you. He wants to build a solid, real, trustworthy, loving, accountable, responsible relationship with you. Are you willing?

This is not a question of whether you are saved. This is about becoming a disciple and abiding in His love in relationship with Him. He promised, "If you abide in My word, you are My disciples indeed. And you shall know the truth, and the truth shall make you free" (John 8:31–32). Do you want to be free? Do you want to be free from your bondage to addiction? Then you must learn to abide. Abiding becomes easier as you dare to learn to trust.

Sitting in the space is the beginning of abiding. Jesus said, "I am the vine, you are the branches. He who abides in Me, and I in him, bears much fruit; for without Me you can do nothing" (John 15:5). Nothing means nothing! You cannot throw off your addiction and be truly free without Him. Learn to sit in the space, bringing your heart to listen.

> *Sit quietly and*
> *Resist your resistance,*
> *Relax your body,*
> *Silence your soul,*
> *Quiet your mind*
> *Swallow your pride,*
> *And soak in the grace of God.*

The results will amaze you. Strength will flow through every fiber of your body. Peace will settle in your mind and heart and eventually God will speak. He will reveal His deep love for you and perhaps tell you what to do next.

God may be silent for a long time. And it may take practice before you can sit in the space long enough to journey through this. God is silent for many reasons, but one of the main ones is that He wants to increase your earnestness. When the men brought the woman caught in adultery and accused her before Jesus, wanting to stone her to death, Jesus was silent. Why? He bent to the ground and wrote in the sand. We don't know what He wrote, but in the silence each man began to see the state of his own soul. They saw their sin clearly before His eyes. When Jesus finally spoke those wonderful words, "He who is without sin among you, let him throw a stone at her first" (John 8:7), the men had already seen their hearts. They now knew themselves and not one could throw a stone.

If God remains silent as you sit in the space, listen to what your heart is telling you. God will show you the state of your own soul. Such a vision may be a surprise and shock to you, but if you allow it to have its work, it will draw you into a deeper sense and level of repentance. This is a work of God; don't run from it. Remain in the space and submit to Him. Through learning to sit in the space and facing what God shows you, by allowing His conviction to melt your heart, you will find a deeper sense of peace and purpose in life. The end result will produce wonderful fruit to enjoy. Remember the fruit of the Spirit is love, joy, peace, longsuffering, kindness, goodness, faithfulness, gentleness, and self-control (see Gal. 5:22–23).

You will need this self-control to overcome your addictive behavior. It is a fruit of the Spirit and not something you can muster with your own strength. Learn to sit in the space and receive what God has to give you!

<u>Getting Real</u>

What do I do to avoid sitting in the space?

What am I afraid of?

Am I willing to try?

What is God telling me?

Chapter Thirteen

CHANGING YOUR HEART

*It is only with the heart that one
can see rightly; what is essential is
invisible to the eye.[1]*
—ANTOINE DE SAINT-EXUPERY

To be able to sit in the space you need to be willing, and to be willing you need a new heart. Your old heart wants to do things its way. It is self-centered, selfish, and very self-protective. It was born under the law and the law is powerless to give life.

> *If there had been a law given which could have given life, truly righteousness would have been by the law. But the Scripture has confined all under sin, that the promise by faith in Jesus Christ might be given to those who believe.*
> —GALATIANS 3:21–22

It is your heart and not the law that is your problem. Jesus said, "Out of the heart of men, proceed evil thoughts, adulteries, fornications, murders, thefts, covetousness, wickedness, deceit, lewdness, an evil eye, blasphemy, pride, foolishness. All these evil things come from within and defile a man" (Mark 7:21–23).

When you were born again God gave you a new heart. He said, "I will give them one heart, and I will put a new spirit within them, and take the stony heart out of their flesh, and give them a heart of flesh, that they may walk in My statutes and keep My judgments and do them; and they shall be My people, and I will be their God" (Ezek. 11:19–20). This new heart was made available when Jesus died on the cross and was given personally to you when you gave your heart to Jesus, asking Him to come into your life. If you have prayed the salvation prayer, you have this new heart.

You may ask, Then why don't I feel like it? What is missing? Why isn't it part of my experience? There is another scripture that helps explain this. God said, "Repent, and turn from all your transgressions, so that iniquity will not be your ruin. Cast away from you all the transgressions which you have committed, and get yourselves a new heart and a new spirit. For why should you die?" (Ezek. 18:30–31).

Once again God's gift of grace is working, but you also need to receive it by faith. This is the part you need to play, the responsibility you must meet. As you already know, you need to deeply repent and turn from behavior you know is wrong, opening your arms in humility to receive by faith what God has to offer. You will receive the benefits of your new heart through obedience.

The bottom line is: The only way to stop addictive behavior is to stop it!

Look over 2 Corinthians 7:11 again and remind yourself of what real repentance looks like. It is not only words, but also actions.

In this process you will discover you are giving your body and self to God as a living sacrifice. Our problem is that we tend to slither off the altar, yet Paul said, "present your bodies a living sacrifice, holy, acceptable to God, which is your reasonable service" (Rom. 12:1). Paul assures us God is only asking something reasonable! This is true when compared to what Jesus endured for us. And it is made possible because "[Jesus] has delivered us from the power of darkness and conveyed us into the kingdom of the Son of His love" (Col. 1:13). It is time to stop making excuses and start putting all you have learned into practice. Get yourself a new heart by doing things God's way in obedience to His Word. Enter into the space and life of your new heart by faith. He will give you the revelation to see this and the grace to obey as you choose to obey one small step at a time. The only way to freedom is through obedience to what God is asking of you. It will not happen by magic. It will happen as your will and God's will come into line and you take hold of the grace He freely offers. God will draw you as you sit in the space and reveal truth to your heart. He supplies the grace to obey. One step of obedience leads to the next revelation and the grace to obey. The next step of obedience leads to the next revelation and the grace to obey, and on it goes one day at a time.

God wants you to be free. This is why He sent His Son to die on the cross in the first place. The question is, Do you want to be free? Are you clinging onto your identity within your addiction? Are you camping around your problems? It's time to face this honestly:

Who are you without your addiction?

Do you know?

Describe yourself.

If you are not sure, find out who you are in Christ, for this is your eternal identity. Here are a few examples:

You are God's child.

> *But as many as received Him, to them He gave the right to become children of God, to those who believe in His name.*
> —JOHN 1:12

You have been justified.

> *Having been justified by faith, we have peace with God through our Lord Jesus Christ.* —ROMANS 5:1

You are a saint.

> *To the saints who are in Ephesus, and faithful in Christ Jesus.* —EPHESIANS 1:1

You are a member of Christ's body.

> *Now you are the body of Christ, and members individually.* —1 CORINTHIANS 12:27

You are complete.

> *For in Him dwells all the fullness of the Godhead bodily; and you are complete in Him, who is the head of all principality and power.* —COLOSSIANS 2:9–10

You cannot be separated from God's love.

> *Who shall separate us from the love of Christ? Shall tribulation, or distress, or persecution, or famine, or nakedness, or peril, or sword?…For I am persuaded that neither death nor life, nor angels nor principalities nor powers, nor things present nor things to come, nor height nor depth, nor any other created thing, shall be able to separate us from the love of God which is in Christ Jesus our Lord.* —ROMANS 8:35, 38–39

You can find grace and mercy in time of need.

> *Let us therefore come boldly to the throne of grace, that we may obtain mercy and find grace to help in time of need.* —HEBREWS 4:16

You are chosen to bear fruit.

> *You did not choose Me, but I chose you and appointed you that you should go and bear fruit, and that your fruit should remain.* —JOHN 15:16

You can succeed with Christ's help.

> *I can do all things through Christ who strengthens me.* —PHILIPPIANS 4:13

God gave you a new heart and wants you to receive it so you can fulfill this destiny. You don't even need to pray for this new heart. If you have prayed the salvation prayer, it is already yours. Receive it by faith in obedience.

> *Receive Jesus Christ to be made sanctification to you in implicit faith, and the great marvel of the Atonement of Jesus will be made real to you. All that Jesus made possible is made mine by the free loving gift of God on the ground of what He performed, my attitude as a saved and sanctified soul is that of profound humble holiness, a holiness based on agonizing repentance and a sense of unspeakable shame and degradation; and also on the amazing realization that the love of God commended itself to me in that while I cared nothing about Him, He completed everything for my salvation and sanctification (see Rom. 5:8)... The effect in me is obedience and service and prayer, and is the outcome of speechless thanks and adoration for the marvelous sanctification wrought out in me because of the Atonement.[2]* —OSWALD CHAMBERS

Accepting your new heart means identifying with Christ within you. God has placed your new heart in you and it is totally in line with God's will. Listen to your new heart. Quiet the old voices, the old desires, the "old man," and listen deeply to what your new heart is telling you. Your new heart knows the mind of Christ.

<u>GETTING REAL</u>

Have I received my new heart?

Am I ready to be obedient to God's directions?

If not, what am I still clinging to?

Who am I in Christ?

Chapter Fourteen

FORGIVENESS AND GOD'S VENGEANCE

Forgiveness is the fragrance the violet sheds
on the heel that has crushed it.[1]
—MARK TWAIN

When facing truth, the losses experienced in life, and coming to the place of repentance, it soon becomes obvious that you are not the only one who is responsible for wrongdoing. There will be many people who have sinned against you, some causing serious harm. What can you do about these people?

In an article written about the issues of survivors of sexual and physical assault by church leaders, Peter Horsfield wrote, "it is too easy to urge forgiveness and reconciliation without first doing the hard work of naming and confronting evil, calling the powerful to account for the abuse of their power, and paying for restitution of those who are victims." He goes on to say that if repentance does not occur and forgiveness demanded then "forgiveness would simply be a condoning of evil."[2]

This flies in the face of teaching in some Christian churches today. You may have been urged many times to forgive, regardless of the response of the offender, and your heart has squirmed, not because you didn't want to forgive, but because somehow it didn't seem right. A careful study of Scripture reveals you are correct. Many Christian writers also recognize this, labeling this unconditional forgiveness as "cheap grace."[3] It heaps guilt on the victim as they fight their feelings of unforgiveness, revenge, and pain, and goes directly against God's own heart and desire for justice.

When you gave your life to Christ your new regenerated heart was built to love what is good and to hate evil (Rom. 12:9) and to enjoy what is lovely (Phil. 4:8). Abuse, violence, fraud, deceitfulness and all sin is worth hating. God hates it too! The Bible even says God hates people who follow a sinful life. "You hate all workers of iniquity. You shall destroy those who speak falsehood; The LORD abhors the bloodthirsty and deceitful man" (Ps. 5:5–6). God does not separate the sin from the sinner as many are fond of suggesting. Otherwise He would send the sin to hell and the sinner to heaven. Instead He keeps the two together and holds the sinner directly responsible for his behavior.

However, when it comes to how you are to treat those who sin against you Jesus said, "love your enemies, bless those who curse you, do good to those who hate you, and pray for those who spitefully use you and persecute you" (Matt. 5:44). Why? "That you may be sons of your Father in heaven; for He makes His sun rise on the evil and on the good, and sends rain on the just and on the unjust" (v. 45).

What do these scriptures mean when looking at forgiveness and how we can offer it to our fellowmen? Jesus gave the answer very clearly in Luke 17:3–4. He said, "If your brother sins against you, rebuke him; and *if he repents*, forgive him. And if he sins against you seven times in a day, and seven times in a day returns to you, saying, 'I repent,' you shall forgive him." Jesus made it clear forgiveness is not unconditional. He said the offender should repent before forgiveness is given.

This is not a new idea. It is exactly how God dealt with you.

You came into relationship with Him by repenting, confessing your sins, and asking for His forgiveness. John the Baptist gave the message, "Repent, for the kingdom of heaven is at hand" (Matt. 3:2), and Peter told the early Christians to "Repent, and let every one of you be baptized in the name of Jesus Christ for the remission of sins; and you shall receive the gift of the Holy Spirit" (Acts 2:38).

The only way into the kingdom of God is through repentance. Forgiveness of your sins is a gift received as a result of God's goodness and grace leading to repentance. Forgiveness does not come cheaply. It cost God the death of His only Son, Jesus Christ, who paid the full price for your sins so that if you follow and believe in Him, you are set free.

God is the only one who ultimately has the power to forgive sins. "The LORD, the LORD God, merciful and gracious, longsuffering, and abounding in goodness and truth, keeping mercy for thousands, forgiving iniquity and transgression and sin, by no means clearing the guilty" (Exod. 34:6–7). You are totally dependent on Him for forgiveness. He will not clear the guilty. Even in Old Testament times repentance was required before forgiveness was given. God provided the means by which His people could be forgiven by the shedding of blood sacrifices by the high priest. Careful rituals ensured God was pleased and the sins atoned for, but sacrifice wasn't enough. The people needed to acknowledge their sins and turn from them.

King Solomon understood the necessity of facing truth and knowing the sin within your own heart as the means of coming to this place of repentance. He said to God, "When each one knows the plague of his own heart, and spreads out his hands toward this temple: then hear in heaven Your dwelling place, and forgive, and act, and give to everyone according to all his ways, whose heart You know (for You alone know the hearts of all the sons of men)...when they come to themselves...and repent...and when they return to You with all their heart and with all their soul…forgive Your people" (1 Kings 8:38–39,47–50).

When Jesus came to Earth He instituted a new covenant that stopped the need for bloody and messy sacrifices by shedding His blood and becoming the full and final sacrifice. He said, "the Son of Man has power on earth to forgive sins" (Matt. 9:6). Jesus not only showed how to have your sins forgiven, but He also told us how to forgive the sins of others who trespass against us (see Luke 17:3). They need to repent first, and only then can be granted the gift of forgiveness. This is reinforced in Ephesians 4:32: "be kind to one another, tenderhearted, forgiving one another, even as God in Christ forgave you." (See also Col. 3:13.) How did God forgive you? Through repentance!

If the offender repents, you are commanded to forgive. It is not a choice. You don't have the option to hold a grudge or take revenge. God has promised to do this for you. "'Vengeance is Mine, I will repay,' says the Lord" (Rom. 12:19). This does not mean you need to confront and seek repentance for every slight misdemeanor. Love is the main objective and you are told, "love will cover a multitude of sins" (1 Pet. 4:8), but in larger issues, the scriptural directive of repentance before forgiveness is essential to maintain integrity in relationships.

What happens when the person does not repent? From the biblical teaching it is clear that forgiveness is not appropriate. Offering "cheap grace" does not honor God, the offender, or yourself. It is only through offering the opportunity for repentance and real change in the heart of the offender that God's love is expressed and the person has the opportunity to enter into a genuine relationship with Him. By pretending the offense is unimportant, or offering forgiveness before there is any change in the offender, you subvert God's will, justice, and love, and put a barrier between the offender and God's truth and righteousness. It is sensible to distrust those who are untrustworthy, to be wary of the violent, and to distance yourself from the possibility of further harm. Distrust is an appropriate response to a traumatic experience of betrayal and you need to protect yourself from those who do harm, until repentance occurs.

The situation may remain unresolved for years. In reality it may never be resolved. In these cases you can avoid a root of bitterness and resentment from poisoning your soul and instead become free and healed from damage if you remain open to the healing work of the Holy Spirit. You must also face the truth, grieve your losses, and wait, preparing your heart for forgiveness. You must enter into the healing process and be willing to forgive. This willingness changes your heart and prevents a root of bitterness from being established. It keeps you in an open position before God and the offender while you wait and see if perhaps God may grant them repentance. This open and loving stance may include confronting or rebuking the person about their sin (see Luke 17:3). Or it may involve cutting off communication to enable the offender to face the harm they are doing, or even initiating legal proceedings.

If you have been hurt very severely you may be thinking, *I can't even be willing!* And here again God comes to your aid. Philippians 2:13 says, "for it is God who works in you both to will and to do for His good pleasure." All you need to do is humbly ask Him to help you even to be willing, and He will. He may help you understand the events and hurts in the offender's life that led to their behavior. He may open your eyes to your own shortcomings. However God chooses to help you, as you humbly submit to His leading, you will gradually notice changes happening until the day finally dawns when you can sincerely declare your heart is willing. It may be a long and painful process, but it is one that will set you free.

No one knows how long you may have to wait to see if the offender comes to repentance, but God can keep your heart soft. Dr. Dan Allender makes the observation that as we wait, God "deepens our hunger for reconciliation by increasing our desire for beauty and perfection—ultimately, our hope of heaven. Hope plays a profound role in our desire for healing…Biblical forgiveness is never unconditional and one-sided…the cost for the offended is in withholding judgment and instead offering the possibility of a restored relationship. The cost for the offender is repentance."[4] This withholding of judgment is the willingness to forgive in the hope that repentance occurs. He goes on to say, "the offender must repent if true intimacy and reconciliation are ever to take place. That means that cheap forgiveness—peace at any cost that sacrifices honesty, integrity, and passion—is not true forgiveness."[5]

Jesus displayed this attitude of willingness to forgive as He was dying on the cross. We know He maintained the power to forgive because He granted forgiveness to the thief who repented on the cross beside Him saying, "Assuredly, I say to you, today you will be with Me in Paradise" (Luke 23:43). But He did not forgive the other thief who did not repent or the multitude who watched His terrible death, even though He possessed the power to do so. Instead He showed His willingness for the multitude to be forgiven if perhaps God should grant them repentance. He left the final decision up to God saying, "Father, forgive them, for they do not know what they do" (Luke 23:34). We know these people had not repented at this time as we are told, "the people stood looking on. But even the rulers with them sneered saying, 'He saved others; let Him save Himself if He is the Christ, the chosen of God.' The soldiers also mocked Him, coming and offering Him sour wine, and saying, 'If You are the King of the Jews, save Yourself'" (v. 35–37). However, when the deed was done, His physical death complete, there was at least one man who may have come to this place of repentance. He was a centurion watching as the atmosphere darkened in the sixth hour, and he called out, "Certainly this was a righteous Man!" (v. 47) Jesus' willingness to forgive and wait, even in the presence of hardened hearts and terrible pain, opened the way for this man's heart to soften and possibly repent. It opens the way granting the same opportunity to all who follow after him, including you and those who have sinned against you.

Jesus gave a severe warning to those who refuse to forgive others after they have repented. In the parable of the unforgiving servant, the man's master forgave him a great debt, just as God has done for you, but then the man refused to forgive those who owed him relatively small amounts even though they had repented and begged for mercy. Because of his actions this servant was delivered "to the torturers until he should pay all that was due to him." And Jesus warned, "So My heavenly Father also will do to you if each of you, from his heart, does not forgive his brother his trespasses" (Matt. 18:34–35). In saying this Jesus did not imply that forgiveness is unconditional. The smaller debtors repented before the unforgiving servant, but he wrongfully refused to accept their repentance and therefore attempted to overrule God's authority. Jesus is always true to God's principles and you must be too.

Forgiveness, then, is not unconditional. It is conditional upon repentance on the part of the offender and needs to be accompanied by a willingness to be open to forgive on the part of the offended. Once the gift of repentance has been offered by God and accepted by the offender and the fruits of repentance have become evident in his life (2 Cor. 7:11), then the transaction is complete. Reconciliation can then occur if it is appropriate. If reconciliation occurs before this, the offender is likely to offend again, because no change of heart has occurred, and this will only cause further harm for all concerned.

What will happen to the person if they refuse to repent? God will take vengeance if and when this is necessary. "It is a righteous thing with God to repay with tribulation those who trouble you" (2 Thess. 1:6). God knows the best strategy and He knows when. We can safely leave this in His perfect hands.

Getting Real

What do I believe the Bible says about forgiveness? Do I need to study it further to find out more?

Who do I need to forgive?

Who do I need to wait for and be willing to forgive?

How can I do this without becoming bitter and resentful?

Should I take revenge?

Who will do this for me?

Chapter Fifteen

GETTING SUPPORT

You are only as sick as your secrets.[1]
—AUTHOR UNKNOWN

To break free from addictive bondage is not an isolated task. You cannot do it on your own. You need fellow believers to encourage, pray for, and walk with you through the difficult and sometimes painful process of change. You need friends and family to be honest and give real feedback about your thinking patterns and behavior. You may even need their help to convince you that you have a problem with addictive behavior at all!

No one is made to live alone. God made you for relationship with Him to bring Him pleasure and for relationship with others. He said, "It is not good that man should be alone" (Gen. 2:18), and this was before sin ever entered the world! He knows your need for human companionship and urges you to acknowledge this. Paul also said, "Let us consider how we may spur one another on toward love and good deeds. Let us not give up meeting together, as some are in the habit of doing, but let us encourage one another" (Heb. 10:24, 25, NIV). Together we can encourage each other to receive God's grace by faith—

enough for each moment, each hour, and each day. No matter how independent, resourceful, and stubborn you have been in the past, becoming free and kicking addiction is something you cannot do on your own. So don't try!

Seek and embrace the help available. If your friends aren't helpful, or if they have the same problem, then it may be wise to change them and find others who will help. If your biological family is not helpful, then draw closer to your church family. If your church family will not help, then find one that will. And don't forget the many organizations, support groups, books, and Christian counselors available. They can all support you in your journey to freedom.

If there is nothing available or suitable in your area, then start a group yourself using this book as a guide! Put an invitation on the local notice board or in the local paper and wait for replies. Use a code name if you are reluctant to use your own. You will be surprised at how many people will appreciate your initiative.

The Bible is full of admonitions to meet together and help one another. Here are a few examples:

Love one another.
—JOHN 13:34

[Submit] to one another in the fear of God.
—EPHESIANS 5:21

We also ought to lay down our lives for the brethren.
—1 JOHN 3:16

If your brother sins against you, rebuke him; and if he repents, forgive him. —LUKE 17:3

Be encouraged, being knit together in love.
—COLOSSIANS 2:2

You need people to uplift, encourage, teach, pray for, and just be with you. Even to bring truth, if you are veering off the rails. Proverbs 27:17 exhorts, "as iron sharpens iron, So a man sharpens the countenance of his friend." As you are sharpened by friends you become more useful to sharpen others in an ever-flowing river of grace.

Proverbs 18:1 speaks of the character traits of one who refuses to mix with others in meaningful relationship and chooses to remain isolated. "A man who isolates himself seeks his own desire; He rages against all wise judgment." Like it or not, the company of others is good for you, even when they do not agree with you, because even here they give you the chance to think clearly, test your ideas and clarify them.

There is another important reason why relationships are so vital. To be real, you need to humble yourself. Confession of your sins and faults to another trusted person will greatly aid your healing process. "Confess your trespasses to one another, and pray for one another, that you may be healed" (James 5:16). James makes confession an essential part of the healing process. And Proverbs 28:13 reminds you, "He who covers his sins will not prosper, But whoever confesses and forsakes them will have mercy." Confession alone, although helpful, is not enough; you must also repent and turn away from your sins to complete the process. It is about walking towards the Light, who is Jesus Christ, where no darkness is found at all (see 1 John 1:5–6). And as you walk in His light, you will find that your fellowship with other believers will improve and you will be healed. "If [you] walk in the light as He [Jesus] is in the light, [you] have fellowship with one another, and the blood of Jesus Christ His Son cleanses [you] from all sin" (1 John 1:7).

If you are still feeling hesitant to seek help, pride may be standing in the way. It may help to realize that hiding the truth will never succeed, because God assures us whatever we do in secret will eventually be exposed. "For there is nothing covered that will not be revealed, and hidden that will not be known"

(Matt. 10:26). How much better to confess your faults, repent, and put things right now instead of having your dirty laundry exposed for all to see!

Few of us like admitting our failures; however, God has extra-special gifts for those who decide to humble themselves. He promises to guide them in justice and teach them His ways (Ps. 25:9); to lift them up (Ps. 147:6); to dwell with them (Isa. 57:15); and to give them extra grace (James 4:6).

GETTING REAL

Am I seeking help from others?

If not, why not?

Who can help and pray for me?

Do I need to join a church fellowship?

Do I need to join an organization or find a counselor?

Do I need to start a support group in my area?

Chapter Sixteen

MAKING HEALTHY CHOICES

It is not hard to make decisions when you know what your values are.[1]
—ROY DISNEY

The effects of addictive behavior on your personality will have severely eroded your ability to use your will effectively. As you are being restored, this part of your soul must also be restored. The first step in achieving this is to bring your will in line with God's will. To initiate this you must submit your will to God.

If you feel you don't want to, ask yourself why. Are you afraid of what God might ask of you? Are you afraid of losing your individuality? Are there things in your life you fear He might ask you to give up? Ask the Holy Spirit to reveal the reasons behind your hesitation and face them before God, bringing them to Him in prayer so that He can change your heart.

If you doubt God has your best interests at heart, then you need to get to know Him more. You can do this by developing your relationship with Him through prayer, reading His living Word, the Bible, and listening to what you think He is saying to you. Write your thoughts in a journal and record answers you receive. There are also many Christian books that can help. Even listening to other people's spiritual experiences and testimonies can deepen your understanding.

If you want to be willing but don't know how because your feelings are not in agreement with your thoughts, remember Philippians 2:13. It says, "for it is God who works in you both to will and to do for His good pleasure." He will help you be willing if you ask Him.

If you do decide to submit your will to God, then pray this simple prayer:

Lord, I submit my will to Your will and ask You to strengthen my will and my ability to use it for Your glory. Please grow the fruit of the Spirit in me rapidly, especially self-control. I ask this in Jesus' name. Thank You.

Now it is time to start exercising your developing will. Throughout the day when you need to make a decision, make a definite decision knowing you are growing your will. If you aren't sure which path to take, pray first and ask God for guidance, get counsel from wise friends, look at your circumstances, and ask yourself what your desires are. These are all relevant in making healthy decisions. Finally make up your mind and choose, believing God is helping you.

God promises to give wisdom to anyone who asks. "If any of you lacks wisdom, let him ask of God, who gives to all liberally and without reproach, and it will be given to him" (James 1:5). James goes on to say you must ask in faith, without doubting (see James 1:6–8).

Learning to use your will effectively and wisely is a growth process. Feed your mind with wholesome material, read your Bible daily, continually filling your spirit and mind with truth. Biblical truth will permeate your soul and spirit and become a guide for you. King David said, "Your word is a lamp to my feet And a light to my path" (Ps. 119:105). He told how this happens, "Your word I have hidden in my heart, That I might not sin against You" (Ps. 119:11). You can hide God's Word in your heart by reading it, thinking about it, considering how it applies to your life, and then considering what you may need to change. God's truth as your guide will help you make wise choices. Over time, as you continually feast on His Word, you will discover you instinctively know what is right and wrong, what is His will and what is not. "The word of God is living and powerful, and sharper than any two-edged sword, piercing even to the division of soul and spirit, and of joints and marrow, and is a discerner of the thoughts and intents of the heart" (Heb. 4:12).

When an occasion arises where you feel like doing something you know is wrong, check your belief system. Two people can experience the same event and yet feel totally different emotions. This is because they believe different premises. For example, imagine two women waiting for a friend to pick them up, and the friend is late. One woman feels fearful and the other annoyed. The fearful woman recently had a friend injured in a car accident and fears this friend may also be hurt. The annoyed woman believes it is impolite to keep people waiting. It is the same event but two totally different emotional responses because of differing beliefs.

If you want to do something you know will grieve God, it may be because you secretly believe you know better than Him, or that your circumstances are somehow different, or that He won't mind if you just do it once. God hates all sin, always, and He holds you responsible for your decisions. Replace false beliefs with the truth, checking your beliefs against the Word of God because this is where the truth is found. Don't worry about your feelings as they will gradually change when your belief system is in order. Psychologist Neil Armstrong points out "It's what we believe that's going to set us free, not what we feel."[2] Your feelings can change with the wind; with the amount of sleep you have or with what you ate for breakfast; but what you believe, if it is the truth, will remain forever.

If you keep on doing the same thing, you will get the same results. Now is the time to start using your will to make healthy choices that will lead you toward a new, exciting, adventurous life with God.

Because God can work in you to change your will to line up with His, you don't need to feel trapped if you don't want to do something you know God wants you to do. Instead ask Him to change your will to line up with His. I have done this in my life over very serious issues, and found it to be true. It can take a little time as you learn to adjust, but God is faithful to His Word.

Healthy choices, one after the other, produce a new life. It does not matter where you start from, or if you feel totally helpless, or even beyond help.

If He could use:
An idolater—Aaron,
A demon-possessed woman—Mary,
A murderer—Paul,
An adulterer—David,
A prostitute—Rahab,
A dead man—Lazarus,
He can use you!

<u>GETTING REAL</u>

Am I making healthy choices? In what areas are my choices not healthy?

Do I want my will to be in line with God's will?

Have I prayed asking Him to line my will up with His?

What can I do today to exercise my will and make a healthy choice?

Chapter Seventeen

FINDING GOD'S VISION FOR THE FUTURE

*You will seek Me and find Me, when
you search for Me with all your heart.*
—JEREMIAH 29:13

God did not create you for a meaningless, boring life. He has good, purposeful, interesting plans for you. "'For I know the plans I have for you,' declares the LORD, 'plans to prosper you and not to harm you, plans to give you hope and a future'" (Jer. 29:11, NIV).

Because God is concerned with every detail, He not only has overall plans, but also daily plans for you: "For we are His workmanship, created in Christ Jesus for good works, which God prepared beforehand that we should walk in them" (Eph. 2:10).

When He created the world and planned your existence, He already knew what He wanted you to do and, if you are willing, He can make it come to pass because He "is able to do exceedingly abundantly above all that we ask or think, according to the power that works in us" (Eph. 3:20).

If you want to know God's plans for you, get alone with Him and ask Him. It is God's pleasure to tell you. He may speak through the Bible, to your spirit, in your dreams, through visions, prophecy, through circumstances, or the wise words of others. He will speak however He wishes. If you are not sure you are hearing from God, then ask Him to confirm it. He wants you to know, even more than you want to hear.

If you think you have an idea, start doing small things that work towards that direction. It doesn't matter how small. It may be saying no to temptation, or saying no to a friend who invites you somewhere questionable. It may be choosing one career over another or changing an unhealthy friendship. It may include reading His Word more, starting a journal, or praying more frequently. It may be getting involved with a ministry at your church or helping someone in need. We progress and mature one step at a time. No one becomes a master pianist with the first thumped chords. It takes practice, self-discipline, and perseverance. But you need the revelation of God's will to begin to change. You may already have it!

"Seek the LORD your God, and you will find Him if you seek Him with all your heart and with all your soul" (Deut. 4:29). The time to do this is now. "Seek the LORD while He may be found, Call upon Him while He is near" (Isa. 55:6).

There is a scripture that says, "Many are called, but few chosen" (Matt. 20:16). I believe this refers to the sad fact that although many are called into various tasks in the kingdom of God, few do the preparation required for these tasks and miss out. Although they may have been called, they were not chosen to fulfill the work. God will call someone else instead. Don't let this happen to you. It doesn't matter where you start. Handley Moule said, "There is no situation so chaotic that God cannot from that situation, create something that is surpassingly good. He did it at the Creation. He did it at the cross. He is doing it today."[1] Ask God for His plans for your life and ask Him to show you the first step to achieve them. One step at a time is all it takes. You will need to take responsibility and persevere through many ups and downs, for this is how character is built.

It is the first step that starts a journey, and if you have chosen the right path, when you get to the end you will hear those wonderful words:

> *Well done, good and faithful servant; you were faithful over a few things, I will make you ruler over many things. Enter into the joy of your lord.* —MATTHEW 25:21

GETTING REAL

Do I know God's vision for my life?

If not, what must I do to find it?

If I do, what am I doing to move toward its fulfillment?

What is my next step?

Chapter Eighteen

SET FREE

If the Son makes you free,
you shall be free indeed.
—JOHN 8:36

If God has spoken to you through this book, you will know it is time to start to change. Change can be a fearful thing, but it can also be very exciting. There is no formula for getting it right and becoming free. The journey is different for everyone. Yet how wonderful this is, because God knows how different each person is. He made you unique and He loves and values you as an individual. He knows your every move, every thought and every desire. He knows how many hairs are on your head every moment. He has counted each one. Pull one out and He knows. Lose one in your comb and He knows. Watch one fly away in the wind and He knows.

A baby learns to walk by first sitting, then often dragging his bottom along the ground, possibly crawling, and then standing on his own two feet. One day the child dares to take that first tentative step. Of course he falls flat on his face, but he doesn't stop. Babies are full of motivation, resilience, and perseverance.

You are told to come into the kingdom of God like a little child. Now is the time to act like a child. A healthy child is precocious, determined, extremely motivated, vulnerable, and trusting. He has a passion for what he wants to do and perhaps even a vague idea of what he wants to be like. He sees his mother or father walking around and somehow he becomes inspired. His thoughts are unlikely to be conscious, but he still catches the vision placed within him instinctively, intuitively by His Father in heaven, even if he cannot vocalize it. God plants the motivation and instinct deep within his soul and the young child moves ahead regardless of the circumstances. Take God's hand and become a little child again. One step at a time is all it takes.

Richard Bach said, "What the caterpillar calls the end of the world the master calls a butterfly."[1] There is a whole world out there to explore, plans to fulfill, people to learn to love, yourself to get to know, and your God who longs to spend time with you. Pray for the revelation you need, ask others to join with you and pray for your freedom. Speak to those who have traveled this road before. Ask your friends and family to help you face truth. Ask the Holy Spirit to reveal truth and convict you of sin, and accept it.

Acknowledge how you have broken God's heart with your behavior and rejection of Him and His ways, and enter deeply into repentance. Produce the fruits of repentance by striving to put things right with God and those you have hurt.

Throw off your old ways and put on the new, walking in the Spirit on the path God has already cleared and prepared for you. Accept that the hard work has already been done by Jesus and walk in this new revelation. Lift your chin. Sniff the fresh air. Stretch out your arms in thanksgiving. You are a child of the Most High God.

Clean up your thinking. Ask friends to help by pointing out unhealthy thinking patterns and replace the lies you believe with truth. The truth is in God's Word, find it and read it. Dig for it like treasure, chew it, and swallow it!

Walk with God through the valley of the shadow of death, not on a shortcut around the edges. Grieve your losses; don't avoid them. Enter into that place of deep pain and bring it before the Lord, for it is He who "heals the brokenhearted And binds up their wounds" (Ps. 147:3).

Learn to sit in the space and take this time as contemplation in God's presence. Be open and willing to hear what the Spirit is teaching you. Listen with your heart as well as your head. Learn to wait, knowing that your waiting will produce magnificent fruit.

Forgive yourself and others who have sinned against you when they repent and, if they don't, place them in God's hands and remain willing to forgive, if they should come to that place of repentance. Keep your heart soft and willing before the Lord and He will bless you.

Pray for the fruit of the Spirit, especially self-control, and ask God to deliver you from temptation. Dare to resist temptation when it does come, relying on your armor, prayer, and God's strength and grace to help you each day. Always look for the way of escape and always take it, even if it hurts, even if it means facing more truth about yourself—for God has given you the escape for a reason. He wants you to be free.

Bring your will into line with God's will, accepting the changes you need to make. Ask God what you need to do next and take that next step. Learn to value simple acts of obedience that lead you closer to God's heart and into the joy He wants to give you. Accept His grace for the ability and power to obey and act on it always.

And step-by-step you will find yourself living a new life in a new kingdom. You will stumble at first, but as your strides gain confidence you will begin to walk, then skip, then hop, and finally run through the fields. You will feel the breeze streaming through your hair and you will hear a strange sound—it is the sound of laughter—and you will be amazed to find the laughter is flowing from your own lips. It has welled up from the depths of your soul and heart, from the very core of your spirit. After all the stumbling, falling, crying, praying, believing, hoping, and waiting, you will finally arrive at this wonderful place. The truth will slowly seep through your consciousness as your spirit soars to meet your Father. For at last you will understand—you are free!

Bibliography

Allender, Dr. Dan B. *Bold Love.* Colorado Springs, CO: NavPress, 1992.

The Amplified Bible. Grand Rapids, MI: Zondervan Bible Publishers, 1964.

Anderson, Neil T. and Mike Quarles. *Overcoming Addictive Behavior.* Ventura, CA: Regal Books, 2003.

Chambers, Oswald. *My Utmost to His Highest.* Grand Rapids, MI: Discovery House, 1935.

The Christian Life Bible, The New King James Version. Nashville, TN: Thomas Nelson Publisher, 1991.

Hamon, Dr. Bill. *Prophets and Personal Prophecy.* Shippensburg, PA: Destiny Image Publishers, 1987.

Holy Bible, New International Version. New York: International Bible Society, 1978.

Horsfield, Peter. "The Church, Forgiveness and Reconciliation." Paper presented to Uniting Church Theological Hall Melbourne.

May, Gerald. *Addiction and Grace.* New York: HarperCollins, 1991.

———. *Will and Spirit.* New York: HarperCollins, 1982.

Merriam-Webster's Collegiate Dictionary, 11th ed.

Nee, Watchman. *The Normal Christian Life.* Carol Stream, IL: Tyndale House Publishers, Inc., 1961.

Payne, Leanne. *The Broken Image.* Grand Rapids, MI: Baker Books, 1981.

———. *Listening Prayer.* Grand Rapids, MI: Baker Books, 1994.

Prince, Derek. *Extravagant Love.* Charlotte, NC: Derek Prince Ministries, 1985.

Schaumburg, Dr, Harry W. *False Intimacy.* Colorado Springs, CO: NavPress, 1997.

Strong, James. *Strong's Exhaustive Concordance of the Bible.* Nashville, TN: Thomas Nelson Publishers, 1997.

Twerski M.D., Abraham J. *Addictive Thinking.* Center City, MN: Hazelden, 1990.

Notes

Introduction

1. Samuel Johnson quote available online at http://www
.dailycelebrations.com/habit2.htm (accessed October 9, 2006).

2. Gerald May, *Will and Spirit* (New York: HarperCollins Publishers,
1982), 40.

Chapter 1: The Truth

1. Richard Bach quote available online at http://www.brainyquote.com/
quotes/quotes/r/richardbac132675.html (accessed October 9, 2006).

Chapter 3: Repentance

1. Luther Burbank quote available online at http://www.quotegarden
.com/thinking.html (accessed October 9, 2006).

2. Taken from *My Utmost for His Highest* by Oswald Chambers.
© 1935 by Dodd Mead & Co., renewed © 1963 by the Oswald Chambers
Publications Assn., Ltd., and is used by permission of Discovery House
Publishers, Box 3566, Grand Rapids MI 49501. All rights reserved.
Quote found on p. 235.

Chapter 4: Putting Off the Old and Putting On the New

1. Leanne Payne, *Listening Prayer* (Grand Rapids, MI: Baker Books,
1999), 52.

2. Watchman Nee, *The Normal Christian Life* (Carol Stream, IL: Tyndale House Publishers, Inc., 1961), 114.

3. *Merriam-Webster's Collegiate Dictionary*, 11th ed., s.v. "Reckon."

4. Nee, *The Normal Christian Life*, 117.

Chapter 6: Through the Valley of the Shadow of Death

1. Henry S. Haskins quote available online at http://www.tomstrong
.org/quotes/q_H.html (accessed October 10, 2006).

2. Chambers, *My Utmost for His Highest*, 205.

Chapter 7: Discovering Your Feelings

1. *Wikipedia*, s.v. "Luc de Clapiers, marquis de Vauvenargues," http://en.wikipedia.org/wiki/Luc_de_Clapiers,_marquis_de_Vauvenargues (accessed October 23, 2006).

Chapter 8: Grieving Your Losses

1. Ralph Waldo Emerson quote available online at http://www.quotegarden.com/risk.html (accessed October 10, 2006).

Chapter 9: Timing

1. Thomas La Mance quote available online at http://www.theotherpages.org/topic-l4.html (accessed October 10, 2006).

2. Copied from *False Intimacy* by Dr. Harry W. Schaumberg copyright 1997. Used by permission of NavPress—www.navpress.com. All rights reserved. Quote found on pp. 28–29.

3. Dr. Bill Hamon, *Prophets and Personal Prophecy* (Shippensburg, PA: Destiny Image Publishers, 1987), 120–123.

4. Copied from *False Intimacy* by Dr. Harry W. Schaumberg copyright 1997. Used by permission of NavPress—www.navpress.com. All rights reserved. Quote found on p. 67.

Chapter 10: God's Grace

1. Gerald May, *Addiction and Grace* (New York: HarperCollins, 1988), 118.

2. Ibid., 16.

3. Ibid., 139.

4. Albert Schweitzer quote available online at http://www.quotationspage.com/quote/4573.html (accessed October 11, 2006).

Chapter 11: Temptation

1. Thomas Babington Macauley quote available online at http://www.citygateassociates.com/character2.html (accessed October 11, 2006).

2. Leanne Payne, *The Broken Image* (Grand Rapids, MI: Baker Publishing Group, 1995), 66.

Chapter 12: Sitting in the Space

1. May, *Addiction and Grace*, 160.

Chapter 13: Changing Your Heart

1. Antoine de Saint-Exupery quote available online at http://www
.brainyquote.com/quotes/quotes/a/antoinedes101532.html   (accessed
October 11, 2006).

2. Chambers, *My Utmost for His Highest*, 294.

Chapter 14: Forgiveness and God's Vengeance

1. Mark Twain quote available online at http://www.quotationsbook
.com/quotes/15555/view (accessed October 11, 2006).

2. Professor Peter Horsfield, "The Church, Forgiveness and Reconciliation." Paper presented to Uniting Church Theological Hall Melbourne.

3. Dietrich Bonhoeffer, *The Cost of Discipleship* (London: SCM Press,
1959).

4. Copied from *Bold Love* by Dr. Dan Allender copyright 1992. Used
by permission of NavPress—www.navpress.com. All rights reserved.
Quote found on pp. 162–165.

5. Ibid., 163.

Chapter 15: Getting Support

1. Quote available online at http://www.quotegarden.com/hmmm
.html (accessed October 11, 2006).

Chapter 16: Making Healthy Choices

1. Roy Disney quote available online at http://quotations.about
.com/cs/inspirationquotes/a/DecisionMaki5.htm   (accessed   October
11, 2006).

2. *Overcoming Addictive Behavior*, by Neil T. Anderson, p. 81. © (2003),
Gospel Light/Regal Books, Ventura, CA 93003. Used by permission.

Chapter 17: Finding God's Vision for the Future

1. Henry Moule quote available online at http://www.geocities.com/memorialoflove2001/flight93heros.html (accessed October 11, 2006).

Chapter 18: Set Free

1. Richard Bach quote available online at http://www.brainyquote.com/quotes/quotes/r/richardbac132675.html (accessed October 9, 2006).

To Contact the Author

Anne Laidlaw
Shiloh Ministries
P.O. Box 26643
Epsom, Auckland 1023
New Zealand
E-mail: shiloh.ministries@hotmail.com